BRINGING UP THE WORLD

How to Finally Focus on What Matters and Watch the Child Bloom

DANIELLE C BAKER

Lucky Book Publishing

To request permissions, contact the publisher at hello@luckybookpublishing.com.

Paperback ISBN: 978-1-7774737-0-9
Hardcover ISBN: 978-1-7774737-7-8
E-book ISBN: 978-1-7774737-8-5

1st edition, December 2024

"If the day ever came when we were able to accept ourselves and our children exactly as we are and they are, then, I believe, we would have come very close to an ultimate understanding of what 'good' parenting means."

– Fred Rogers

MY GIFT TO YOU

I am so glad you're here!

As my Gift to you, get FREE Access to the Audiobook of Bringing Up the World and other Free Book Bonuses by scanning the QR Code below or visiting https://beingconnected.ca/book

---

PRAISE FOR
BRINGING UP THE WORLD

Nurturing Children, Strengthening Communities

Bringing Up the World" offers a fresh and empowering take on parenting. With its core message that "it takes a village," this heartfelt guide restores parental confidence, emphasizes compassion, and inspires meaningful, positive change for every child. This heartfelt guide is a must-read for anyone committed to helping children.

   - *Shelley A Mudock, Best-Selling Author, HEALTHY & FIT FOR LIFE*

Breaking the Cycle for Future Generations

Oh wow, I was hooked from the beginning. Passing down childhood trauma from generation to generation, this right there made me wish I had this book before I had my daughter. Thank you Danielle! Every parent should read this book.

   - *Nadee Fernando-O'Driscoll, Author, Labyrinth of Dreams*

Expert Strategies, Heartfelt Lessons

Danielle's years of experience shine in this guide,

offering gentle yet transformative strategies for raising children who can change the world.

> - *Charles Achampong, Keynote Speaker, Author of Around the World in Family Days*

The Village Every Parent Needs

Packed with actionable insights and heartfelt wisdom, this book is the village every parent needs to help their child bloom and grow.

> - *Manali Haridas, CEO, Zen for You & Author of "You Got This Mom*

A Lifeline for Parents, Especially the Overwhelmed

Being a parent is hard. The sentence "it takes a village " really applies, especially to those carrying the weight of both as a single parent. Danielle brings real life to one of the hardest jobs and if there were any book on parenting I would recommend to first time parents or those being hard on themselves, this is it!

> - *Heather Coleman, TEDx Keynote Speaker and Author - Our Money Narrative*

Clear, Compassionate, and Powerful

Danielle Baker seamlessly combines expert advice with heart, offering a clear, compassionate roadmap for parents and caregivers who want to make a meaningful difference.

> - *Cristie Vito, Keynote Speaker and Author - Bless the Meds*

It's Never Too Late to Parent with Purpose

Where was this book 13 years ago? I have done core value exercises before, but somehow missed the big picture: what am I doing in my every day life to instill MY most important values into the one most important vessel in this world: my only child. How did I miss it? And yet in this book, it took me a chapter to get it. If I got that much in one chapter, imagine what the rest did for me. Get this book! Invest your resources - money, time, kisses - in the right place. It wasn't too late for me with a tween in my house. It isn't too late for you wherever you are on this life path.

> - *Rosy, the Mortgageless Mentor, Author, Don't Have Sex Nine Months Before Christmas and other Practical Financial Tips*

It Takes a Village—And a Vision

Danielle masterfully reminds us that raising a child is not just a family effort but a community act that has the power to ripple across the world.

> - *Sarah Boyd, Holistic Lifestyle Coach*

A Guide to Global Change Through Parenting

Danielle Baker's guide transforms parenting into a powerful act of global change. A must-read for anyone who believes in the magic of nurturing children to create a better world.

> - *Fran Garton, Pain Reduction Coach, Fibromyalgia Warrior and Body-Positive Trainer*

A Game-Changer for Modern Parenting

A refreshing take on modern parenting that emphasizes self-awareness, community, and intentional action. A game-changer for raising confident, happy children.

- Richa Rehan, Physiotherapist, Best-selling Author, Things Every Girl Should Know About Her Body

Shape the Future, One Child at a Time

With practical tools and profound wisdom, Danielle C Baker inspires us to shape the future—one resilient, supported child at a time.

- Teri Kingston, TEDx Speaker Coach, Best-selling Author, Get Ready for TED When TED is Ready for you!

A Must-Read for Future Parents and Beyond

Danielle's book is an incredible guide for anyone preparing to parent or seeking to heal their inner child. Her insights on childhood trauma and self-healing offer wisdom for parents and non-parents alike. A truly inspiring, compassionate resource for creating a better future where we put the child first.

- Ellie Laliberté, Best-Selling Author, Letters From You to You: Awaken Your Power Through Conversations With Your Higher Self

DEDICATION

I dedicate this book to my sons, Donnic and Daylan.

I know what you two are thinking so let me publicly specify that I am not naming you in order of preference. This is solely a chronological thing! LOL

We are taught that the most important role as a parent is to keep our children safe. My experience with you two has taught me that, quite often, our children come into this world to save us.

Donnic, you came in and saved me from the world around me. Daylan, you came in and saved me from myself. For that, I will forever be grateful that you both chose me.

So to you, Daylan and Donnic (I'm just messing with you now!), I thank you for making me a better person and know that I am proud of the outstanding men you have become.

ACKNOWLEDGEMENT

I am taking an unconventional approach to the traditional Acknowledgement protocol by placing it at the front of this book. I owe my deepest gratitude to many people who have helped me get my work published and I do not want their contribution to be lost and overlooked at the end.

I also find that naming a long list of people would not do it justice. I choose not to name people individually as I would inevitably forget someone.

I will start off by thanking the thousands of children and their families that I have had the honour of working with for giving me the solid knowledge and resources I have acquired from my 20+ years experience in the field of Early Childhood Development and Education. You have taught me more than Academia ever will.

I started writing this book with the best of intentions and then, as the book was close to completion, I started to panic and retreat. The inevitable question kept popping up in my mind: "Who am I to write a book on parenting?"

It took me a couple of weeks to write the book and a couple of years to complete it.

During this time of internal struggle, I got to see who was genuinely rooting for me. I can honestly count on two hands the people who continuously backed me up, encouraged me, and motivated me to get the work done.

I wish to acknowledge my "Day Ones," the individuals who were cheering me on the moment I announced I was writing this book and who have not stopped cheering me on since. You know who you are.

I also want to thank the ones who I have met along the way, giving me a wealth of encouragement and support to get this book out.

Your occasional mention of the book over coffee, your kind messages and follow up texts, and your much needed swift kicks in the behind helped me get through with it. This book has opened up my eyes to seeing where my real support is. Blood or not, you know who you are and I love every single one of you.

And, of course, I want to thank Lucky Book Publishing for supporting me in making this a reality.

"To my children, I'm sorry for the unhealed parts of me that in turn hurt you. It was never my lack of love for you. Only a lack of love for myself."

- Teresa Shanti

AUTHOR'S NOTE

Before becoming a mother, I spent many years working with children and their families. However, without first hand parenting experience, my advice was often based on theory rather than real life. Parenting has taught me that true understanding comes from lived experience.

My children, Donnic and Daylan, have been my greatest teachers and motivators, pushing me to heal and break generational patterns. While I regret not always being fully present for them during the times I was in survival mode, this has deepened my empathy for both children and the adults who care for them.

Writing this book is my way of helping parents show up for their children as they truly need, regardless of their life's challenges. My work has shifted from focusing solely on supporting children to empowering the parents who support them. By building up parents, we create a better world for the next generation.

This book aims to restore parents' confidence as their child's primary educators and to unify the child's community. Together, we can make a lasting impact, one child at a time.

"...And these children

That you spit on

As they try to change their worlds

Are immune to your consultations.

They're quite aware

Of what they're going through..."

- David Bowie

MY DREAM

One of my dreams is to change the world, one child at a time, by strengthening the connections that children need to thrive: connections between parents, teachers, and their communities. Can you help?

Please reach out if you would like me to speak to your audience about any of the following themes:

- Building stronger parent-child relationships through understanding and connection.

- Identifying and supporting children's learning styles to ensure academic success.

- Recognizing and nurturing play patterns to support early development.

- Designing the right support system for children and their families to thrive.

- Finding work-life balance and aligning values in leadership roles.

- Integrating self-care practices for parents, teachers, and professionals.

https://beingconnected.ca/about

TABLE OF CONTENTS

INTRODUCTION

"Bringing Up the World" emphasizes the profound impact our interactions with children have on our communities and the world. The values we instill in our children shape their futures and their influence on society.

When I refer to "parents," I mean anyone who interacts with children, whether they are biological parents, teachers, doctors, neighbours, or even strangers. Children learn from observing all of us, and our actions set the example they follow.

In this book, "your child" can refer to your own child, your student, patient, coworker's child, or any child watching you. It is about recognizing the influence we have and holding ourselves accountable for our actions towards and around children.

The chapters are structured based on my 20+ years of experience in the world of Early Childhood Development and Education to ensure success for both you and the children in your life. Mastering each subject in the sequence presented in this book is crucial to breaking harmful patterns and avoiding the pitfalls of traditional approaches that have failed children for generations.

"Bringing Up the World: How to Finally Focus on What Matters and Watch the Child Bloom" is a guide to shifting our focus back to the child. By doing so, we can address long-standing issues in our education and social systems and create a better world.

Welcome to YOUR Village!

"Children are not things to be molded, but are people to be unfolded."

- Jess Lair

PART 1:
GETTING CLEAR ON WHAT YOUR CHILD REALLY NEEDS

The next three chapters will help you find the distinction between your needs and your child's needs. As parents, we are not taught to tell the difference, and that line is often blurred.

We often provide our children with the help and attention WE lacked as children, as opposed to providing them with the help and attention THEY need as unique individuals.

Separating your needs from your child's needs will allow you to clearly see how to show up for your child.

This is where my 20+ years of experience in working with thousands of children and their families come into play. As I guide you through the next three chapters, you will quickly see that I do not take a conventional approach to parenting because there is no such thing as a "cookie-cutter" approach to parenting.

There is no magic formula that will solve everyone's parenting problems because there is nothing generic about raising children. I will even go as far as urging you to stay away from anyone who will give you advice on how to parent your child without having gotten to know you and your child first.

It is now time to figure out exactly what Parenting will look like for you.

"Our heritage and ideals, our code and standard - the things we live by and teach our children - are preserved or diminished by how freely we exchange ideas and feelings."

- Walt Disney

CHAPTER 1:
GETTING TO KNOW THE
PARENT YOU WANT TO BE

Contrary to what most Parenting books, articles, podcasts, and other publications will tell you, this all starts with putting the focus on you first.

With the title of this book and what I have described in the Introduction, some of you will be asking: "If the focus is to be put on the child, why do I have to do the work first?"

The answer to that is straightforward and applicable to the broader definition of "parents" described in the Introduction. If you are not clear on what is important to you, what you stand for, and what you want to pass down to your future generations then you will be slushed around the parenting world like a boat lost at sea without a rudder.

If you are not aware of the childhood pain and trauma you are potentially passing down to your child, then all you are doing is strengthening the generational patterns that need to be broken.

In short, if you do not address your childhood traumas, your parenting will.

How to know if you are a great parent

My father, who was a child's psychologist for 40+ years, once told me something that stuck with me as a parent. I am translating and paraphrasing what he said here with this statement:

"The only way you will know that you were a great parent is if your children surpass you in life".

Allow yourself to let this sentence sink in for a moment. How comforting is it to know that there is a defined way of confirming that you did well as a parent, even when you are not convinced that you did.

Now I am going to shake you up a little and ask: How will you be able to tell if your child surpassed you if you do not know who you are? What is the reference point?

This is where the work begins...

Identifying your true values

What values are important to you? Do those values represent you or are you abiding by the ones that were imposed on you as a child? Are you living by your values? How do they show up in your day-to-day life, personally, professionally, socially, and spiritually?

Not having direct answers to these questions will destabilize you not only as an individual but as a parent as well.

So I ask you: "What are your Core Values?"

I know this may sound strange but, even though most people know what a Core Value is, many are unable to identify their own. And if they are able to identify them, many will realize that they are not putting them into practice on a day-to-day basis.

If I was to ask you to identify your top 5 Core Values, would you be able to answer right away? Or would you need some time to look it up to remind yourself what a Core Value is (which is what I had to do)?

By asking these questions, my clients and my students quickly realize that, although they know what a value is, they do not know what THEIR values are. Why is that? I was one of those people a few years ago. I have studied social sciences and human development for decades and I could not put a name to my values. It was only when I stopped to think about it carefully (and googled it a little) that I started to understand what a Core Value really is and which ones I resonated with.

That is when it hit me that not teaching children about values and how to live with them is doing us a lot of harm as a society. We are forced to live by other people's values and are then left to fend for ourselves, not understanding the impact those values have on our lives.

Now let us hone in on your true Core Values...

There are various types of values. Core Values are what make you who you are, your essence so to speak. The first ones you are unknowingly introduced to are the cultural/generational values you were raised with, passed down from previous generations and from your community. As you grow older, you find that some of these values do not serve you well, but you are still sticking to them because that is just how it is. You will also find professional/business values, spiritual values, and social values, which makes it even more difficult to determine which ones are your actual values.

It is important to assess your values periodically to see whether they still hold true for you. Most of the time they do because they are your Core Values. They represent who you are and how you want to show up in life. But, sometimes, you will find that you need to adjust them, according to the experiences that occur in your life.

My father once explained to me his views on what a Core Value is. His words resonated with me as I was teaching a course in College on the influences of family and community in a child's life. At the time, I was trying to paint the right picture to define values for my students.

What he shared with me helped me understand how values should be used once we have identified them. It is great to be able to name our values, but then what? What are we supposed to do with them? This is how my father explained values to me:

Human needs and rights are negotiable. Someone can make the decision that you only need 48 oz of water a day instead of 64 oz a day and, as long as you are still getting water, you are okay. Our needs and rights are constantly being changed and negotiated, now more than ever. But values, those are non-negotiable. No one can tell you who you are and what you should believe in. No one has the right to tell you that what you truly believe in is wrong because it is who you are at the Core.

That was the visual I needed to understand how to use Values to determine our non-negotiables. My father's explanation has also been appreciated by the individuals I have worked with or taught on the subject.

As life progresses, you come across other types of values. They will work in tandem with your Core Values, depending on the role you are taking on. At work, for instance, teamwork, creativity, and cooperation would become the more dominant values. Other values will also show up when it comes to your contribution to your community, religious group, and social circles. They are not necessarily your Core Values, but you will work them into your day-to-day to help you move forward in life.

Those secondary values are important but will change according to certain life circumstances. This is why it is important to do an occasional decluttering of your values in order to stay clear and focused on how you show up authentically in life. Businesses review their organizational values with their strategic planning sessions every 3 to 5 years in order to keep the business moving forward. It only makes sense we do the same with our own personal values.

Your Core Values will hardly ever change, unless an important event occurs in your life, changing your outlook on your reality. Values can and will however, get slightly modified along the way. You will know when it is time to declutter your Core Values, your boundaries, and your non-negotiables (deal breakers). The things that you usually look forward to in your life and the things that usually keep you motivated will start to weigh you down. You will start dreading going to work when you used to be happy to go to work. You will start dreading getting together with certain friends and family members because you feel exhausted after you meet with them. These are all signs that something is no longer in alignment with your Core Values. That is your sign that it is time to investigate what needs to change, whether it is your routine, jobs, or people in your life.

For the purpose of demonstrating how a modification of a value looks like, let us say that one of my Core Values is Tradition. I have set my life's course and my boundaries around the fact that my family traditions will remain an integral part of my life. Now let us imagine that I meet my life partner who also holds family traditions as a value. I now find myself having to make modifications as my partner becomes an integral part of my family. Respecting the fact that I cannot disregard my partner's family traditions and that I will not allow my partner to disregard mine, we now find ourselves incorporating each other's family traditions in our day-to-day lives. This does not change our Core Values, it simply changes how they show up in our life together. Neither one of us has discarded our Tradition Value, we simply made it fit into our new reality.

How your values influence your parenting style

Once you get clear on your Core Values and make them authentically part of who you are, you are in a better position to have them show up in your outside world. In order for you to understand how you show up as a parent, you need to understand and identify your Core Values. They will guide you through your parenting experience.

They will also trigger you as a parent. When your values are not respected or are threatened, you will react almost instantly. Usually in a negative way. I refer to these as parental triggers.

By knowing your Core Values, you will know and understand what is important to you as a parent. These values become your non-negotiables when it comes to making decisions that will affect your child. They will not only help you to see what is required of you when it comes to making a decision for your child but they will also help you understand why you react a certain way when it comes to your child.

By paying attention to your reactions when your values are compromised, you will be able to see what changes you need to make in your life to fully show up as a parent. I can take this even further and say that these reactions are also what indicate the parts of you that need to heal in order to prevent passing on your generational baggage to your child.

The importance of decluttering your values

When you are at work and any other social setting, your Core Values will also help you understand why some people rub you a certain way and learn how to make the necessary adjustments to make it easier for you in these environments. This will help you greatly in understanding why some of the parents you will come in contact with through your child will delight you, and some will irritate you for no reason. There actually is a reason: how their actions align (or not) with your values.

When addressing issues related to values, the number one rule is to remember that they are non-negotiable. No one can tell you that your values are wrong, and you are certainly not entitled in any way to tell others that theirs are worthless. That includes children's values as well. Yes, children have their own values, even if we do not teach them about values. We cannot get caught up in imposing our values on others because there is no way we would allow others to impose theirs on us. This rule applies to our children as well.

The great thing about going deep in identifying your Core Values is that you quickly realize that, no matter the upbringing, the environment, the cultural and religious backgrounds, or the socio-economic demographics, Core Values are almost always the same from one person to another. We are really not that different from one another. We are all looking to be loved and to be respected. So why do we turn against each other? The answer is simple... we are not taught to understand what values are and how to use them.

Where the work begins...

I am going to put you to work in this section! It is a longer exercise but it is THE exercise that will make everything else in this book come together. You must invest a little time with this one to work out the rest of the book with ease. It will be worth it, not only with the decision-making as a parent, but with every other aspect of your life. This work can take weeks to get through so give yourself the time you need. It is not possible to rush through this.

You can do this exercise by following the steps enumerated below or by signing up for the mini-course I have created on Core Values. I am giving free access to this mini-course to those who are supporting my work by reading this book. You will find the information on how to access my mini-course on Cores Values for free at the end of this chapter.

EXERCISE - GETTING TO KNOW THE REAL YOU

1. Identify your top 5 Core Values, the ones you identify with the most. You can look up values on the internet or have me guide you through them by signing up for my mini-course on Core Values. Any internet search on values will give you a long list to choose from. Select those you resonate with the most and then narrow down your list to the 5 most important ones.

2. Identify the top 5 values you were raised with. Which ones were imprinted on you by your parents, your teachers, your religious leaders, your community? This helps you get a better picture of where you come from.

   If you are not certain which values were imposed on you as a child, ask your parents, grandparents, or other family members what values they were raised with. There is a good chance those were the same values you grew up with.

3. Which ones of your Core Values do you want to pass down to your child? At the end of the day, what are the ones you want your child to have? This will help you gauge how well you are handling parenting. Do you expect your children to live with your values even if their life's course does not follow yours?

4. What are the values at your workplace? Your place
    of worship? Your circle of friends? (The workplace
    is easier to identify as the organizational values will
    be listed in the mission statement). Do you align
    with these values? Does your organization's day-
    to-day operations reflect these values? Do your
    spiritual leaders "practice what they preach"? Does
    the congregation live by these values daily, even
    when no one is watching? Do your friendships and
    relationships uplift you or drain you?

    *Review these regularly to be sure you are living by your
    Core Values. Generally, when things start feeling off and
    out of balance in your life, it is because something does
    not align with your values. That is your indication that
    you need to review how your values show up in your
    day-to-day life.*

5. Now that you have identified your Core Values (and
    the secondary values that show up in your external
    world), start looking at whether or not you are living
    by them. Do your actions, decisions, and way of life
    align with your Core Values?

    *Here is an example to help you determine if your values
    shows up in your day-to-day life:*

    *Family is an important value for you. However, you work
    70 to 80 hours a week, bringing work home, keeping*

you away from your family. Are you really living by your Core Family Value? Do you feel guilty about missing family events? Do you feel like you are slowly burning out? Do you find that there is more tension between you and your partner because of your work schedule? Those will be your indications that you are out of balance with your Core Value.

6. Start looking at the changes you need to make in your life to make sure your values show up authentically. Using the example of the Family Value given in the previous question, it would not be reasonable to simply quit your job on the spot. There are many other factors to take into consideration. This is where you will need to get creative on finding ways to reduce your workload.

   Go over each of your Core Values and identify where your lifestyle does not align with them. Where do you need to make changes in your life in order to align with your Core Values? Look at your home life, your work life, your social life, and your spiritual life.

As you work on this exercise, do not be too hard on yourself; it may feel overwhelming. Do not give up! It can take weeks for you to sort through it all. Just like decluttering your home, cleaning up your values will take time and may get messier before it starts looking and feeling good.

Remember that this will be a game-changer for you. Once you understand what fuels you and what makes you who you are, nothing and no one will be able to put out your fire. More importantly, by being clear on your non-negotiables, you will be able to trust the decisions you will make regarding your child, as long as your child's best interest is at the front of the decision-making process.

Do not forget that I am here to help and support you. Here is the information on the course I am giving you access to, should you like me to guide you through this exercise. Get all the information at https://beingconnected.ca/book

"The best brains of the Nation may be found in the last benches of the classroom."

- A. P. J. Abdul Kalam

CHAPTER 2:
GETTING TO KNOW
HOW YOUR CHILD LEARNS

Finding out how your child learns will be the best tool you will ever have as a parent. You are the primary educator for your child. You are the resource teachers need to ensure your child's academic success. Knowing exactly what learning support your child needs will allow you to make decisions regarding your child's academy journey with confidence.

People are always surprised when I tell them that I struggled in school. I was the quiet kid in class who was always willing to help, who always did the work, always had great grades, and never disrupted the class. I recently decluttered my house and found a school memorabilia box that my mom had made for me. It had every single report card, from kindergarten to grade 12!

As I started looking over them, I noticed the teachers' comments on some of them. They all had the same generic comments about my academic performance: I was essentially the student every teacher wanted in their class. So why was school hard for me?

I will start off by saying that it is while writing this book that I started to share how I struggled in school. Because of my academic results, I was ashamed to speak up about it. When I did say something about how difficult it was for me, I was always given the same answer: "You're a smart kid; you'll figure it out!" Or people assumed I was only looking for attention.

Yes, I could figure it out, even at a young age. But that did not mean I did not need some explanations, guidance, or even reassurance. Having been flagged as the student who did not need assistance with her school work, I was left on my own to struggle with the subject matters.

I would not dare talk about my struggles with my friends since I knew that would make me look and sound pretentious. Many of them were struggling with their grades, getting punished at home for their struggles, and being bullied by their teachers in class. So I knew that I would get backlash for saying I was having a hard time.

After reading this chapter so far, many may be asking why I would be bringing this up. This silent struggle of mine is very common amongst the "high performing" students. The reason for my struggling in school is very simple: I do not learn things the way they were taught in school.

Why school is a waste of time to most

Sitting at a desk, not moving, not making a sound, just reading and listening to the teachers talk to the board is not how I learn. In fact, that is not how anyone learns.

I am mentioning how I learn here in order to help you understand how the education system has been failing students for decades. I can never fit in the "cookie-cutter" way of learning, and neither does any other student.

I need to ask questions, I need to manipulate things, I need to try the concepts for myself, I need to fail miserably at it, to make a mess, and to learn from all those mistakes. That is just how my brain works. Having worked in schools for over 20 years, I can confirm that this is how most students will learn best.

Here is more information I have never shared until now: I was diagnosed with "giftedness" early on in elementary school. Having been diagnosed in the 80s, this "title" could simply have been given to me because I did not have meltdowns and was not "non-verbal." In my adult years, I have since been tested 5 more times and the results are still not clear, which baffles the specialists. Essentially, we do not know what I have, but I have something! I decided to bring this up in this book to explain my point of view on neurodiversity.

Neurodiversity serves a purpose for Neurotypical people who need an absolute reason for someone not to fit in the box they want them to fit in. This allowed me to come to the conclusion that a diagnosis does not define who I am. I am who I am.

While the specialists struggled to label me with an "acceptable" identity in order to make everyone more comfortable with why I could not fit in a box when it came to learning, I embraced who I am and decided to help children love and accept themselves for who they truly are. I then shifted to the parents to help them support their child and to be more confident with the decisions they will have to make concerning schools.

I will admit this is something that is extremely hard to explain in writing. It is also the very first time I talk about my so-called "condition." It was something we could not talk about in the past.

This leads me to why school was a waste of time for me. I am a visual learner with a photographic memory.

I need to see something for my brain to register what I am learning. This means that spending a day in class, with a teacher talking about a concept without an actual visual for it, could not work for me. There was nothing there for my brain to take a picture of. The only way I could process the information in that scenario was to doodle in my notebook. While listening to the teacher, my brain could associate my drawings to the topic discussed, and I could then remember the drawing to remember the lessons. However, a child doodling in a book while the teacher is speaking was, and still is, considered disrespectful. So my notebook and pencil were taken away and I now, once again, found myself "blind" to the knowledge I was being taught.

I had to wait until I got home and teach myself. Yes it worked, yes I figured it out, but can we all agree that it was taking me much more time this way? In order to maintain my "high achieving" student status, I had to do the work twice!

If I was doing my learning once I got home, what was the point of going to school?

The change that needs to happen in schools

That is the question EVERY child asks themselves.

All I needed to end the struggle was to be allowed to doodle while the teacher talked. Or have the teacher show a picture once in a while. But the rigid teaching techniques of our education system could not allow it at the time.

> *This brings me to the most important step to*
> *fully allow a child to bloom:*
> *How do they learn?*

I am focusing on how children learn in this chapter as opposed to elaborating on personality traits for a very specific reason. You know your child. You know your child's personality, what sets them off, and what calms them down. There are endless books and other resources on knowing your child. But it is not your child's personality that will determine how they process information.

There are hardly any resources on what to do with your child's play patterns and learning styles. In fact, teachers are not taught how to observe a child's play patterns and how to incorporate all learning styles in their lesson plans because play is not an integral part of teaching in our current Education system.

Why do I think that is more important to address than figuring out the "Colours" of your child's personality? It is not only because the most traumatizing years of your child's life will be during his or her academic years. It is also because if you know your child's play patterns and learning styles from birth, you will know exactly how to help him or her develop fully in the very crucial early years.

So how do children learn?

What is their way of remembering things and processing new information? As adults, we know what works for us and what does not. That is why we become the best resources for our children.

Children are not told that people learn differently when they are in school. They are simply told that they must learn the way the school teaches. Even parents are pressured into teaching their child the way they are taught in school. Any parent of my generation who has to sit with their child and try to help them with the "new math" understands what I mean here.

The only way to set up a child for success in their academic years is to respect their learning styles when teaching them new concepts. This does not require additional work or energy since these learning styles show up as early as your child's first year. This does, however, require you to be present with your child and pay attention to how he or she interacts with you and others as an infant.

What to look out for

How do they respond to their environment? How do they respond to you? When you call their name, do they stop moving, make noise, and wait to hear your voice again (auditory)? Do they turn their head to look in the direction of your voice (visual)? Do they start cooing back at you (verbal)? Do they reach their hands and/or feet out towards you to try to touch you (manual)? Do they start kicking and flapping their arms around (kinesthetic)?

These reactions do not necessarily set their learning types in stone, but they are a great indicator of a useful approach to aid their development at a very early age. When you do a quick search on the internet about the different learning types, you will find different categories. Some will say there are 4, some will say there are 6, 8, 11, and so on, depending on the theorists you are reading.

The actual number of ways to learn is not important, as we almost all have a combination of more than one learning style. This is why it is not beneficial to try to get ourselves and our children to fit into only one learning type.

Understanding 6 main learning styles

The key thing to remember is that we have a primary or dominant learning style, complemented by secondary ones. Understanding this puts you ahead of the game when trying to help support your child through their learning years.

Here are the main learning styles you should focus on with your child. There are many more, but, through my years of experiences working with children and adults, everyone will fall under one or more of these categories. While reading through these, see if you can recognize yourself in any of them:

- Visual: responds to pictures, graphs, diagrams, images, spatial understanding, etc.

- Auditory: responds to sounds, music, rhythms, etc.

- Cognitive/logical: responds to logic, reasoning, systems, sequences, numbers, etc.

- Kinesthetic/physical: responds by using hands, body, sense of touch, acting things out, etc.

- Verbal: responds to words (both written and spoken), vocabulary, acronyms, etc.

- Social: responds to group settings to learn new things, explaining what was learned to a group, etc.

- Solitary: responds to self-study, prefers to be alone, etc.

The last two are extremely important to identify once in school. If the child is a solitary learner, group work or "free study" in class will be torture for them. For a social learner, isolating them to "stop interrupting the class" will only make things worse. If your child is a social learner, you would have noticed the negative impact the "distance learning" format had on your child during the pandemic. If your child is a solitary learner, this virtual format would have been beneficial to them. You may have found out that your child was doing much better with school work when at home.

Getting everyone back on the same team

It is just as important for teachers and educators to know each student's learning types. In order to help the children succeed in school, parents need to share this information with their child care providers and their children's school. Knowing your child's learning styles from birth, you are the best resource for teachers in knowing how to create the classroom your child needs. Schools should be requesting this information in the registration progress.

That simple question would open up communication between parents and educators and build a trusting relationship, which will, in turn, ensure support for every child. Some may see this as "extra work" and yes, it may feel like it at first. But when you look at how much time we will be saving from unnecessary negative behaviours, missed assignments, etc., we would actually be saving a lot of time and unnecessary stress.

The change that saves time and energy

Changing our teaching methods to match each student's learning type is not extra work. In fact, it takes a workload off the teachers since they no longer have to "guess" what will work and spend the majority of the class time managing disruptive behaviours. The students and their parents will have done the majority of the prep time for the teachers.

There is no extra work and energy involved in allowing a child to stand up while working. There is however a lot of extra work in getting a child to sit still in class.

There is no extra work involved in allowing a child to doodle in a notebook or not maintain eye contact with the teacher while he or she is teaching. However, there is a lot of extra work involved in lecturing the student on how you think they are disrespecting you.

As adults, I challenge you to sit in a meeting or at your desk without making a sound, without moving around in your chair, and without looking away from your work during your entire shift. Most of you will last but a few minutes, maybe even a few seconds. How realistic is it for us to categorize children as "difficult" for not being able to do it for 6.5 hours?

One major change that needs to be made in our education systems is the assumption that students who can quietly sit still for 6.5 hours a day in class do not face developmental struggles. If we can admit that it is impossible for anyone to sit still at full attention for that long, then how are we not questioning or testing the children who can?

Easy changes that can be made today

I understand that teachers and educators will be on the defensive with some of the points I mention in this chapter. I can confirm this by referring to the number of comments, complaints, and rants that go on within the teaching communities when the subject of making changes to improve classroom management is brought up.

Although the majority of teachers are constantly looking to find the right formula to apply in their classroom to make things better for every one of their students, they are so burned out, discouraged, and overwhelmed that they can only see what is burning them out and overwhelming them.

Before you view this chapter as unrealistic, allow me to share some quick, simple, and budget-friendly ideas for how to adjust some teaching methods to accommodate each learning style. Note that these ideas work well in traditional public or private schools, in home/micro/pod schools, in childcare centers and after school programs, and in any other form of educational structure:

- Visual: add images to your handouts and require less writing of notes. If speaking, use descriptive language or examples (for example, say things like: "think of a green leaf, imagine a red balloon, etc."). Let them doodle!!!!! They are not disturbing the class.

- Auditory: play soft music in the background; make up rhymes or songs as you teach. Have the students play a beat while you talk.

- Kinesthetic: Choose your kinesthetic students for demonstrations in class, offer materials they can manipulate while you teach, have tennis balls and/ or foam rollers available for them to roll under their feet during "quiet work."

For more examples on the other learning styles mentioned in this chapter, please refer to my website: www.beingconnected.ca/learning

YouTube - Visit the "Teacher's Corner" Playlist on my YouTube channel: https://www.youtube.com/playlist?list=PLmMQJZNTAyVU14aDyR3P-TuW4IMeXS7Id

Where the work begins...

The following exercise will help parents get to know what kind of learner their child is. By knowing this, you become the resource that will help your child get the best out of school and the trusted person the school can turn to to help your child throughout his or her academic years.

For teachers, this exercise will help you get to know the learning styles of every one of your students and what teaching tools you need to bring in for that particular school year. This will also help you gain parents' trust by addressing their child's individual needs. Parents will automatically know that you are paying attention to their child, and this will help open up the lines of communication when more challenging conversations need to happen.

EXERCISE - GETTING TO KNOW THE REAL CHILD

1. What does your child like?

Not what you think he or she likes. A baby is not born obsessing over superheroes and princesses. Of course they will learn to like them. These whimsical characters were designed that way strategically, but those are forced passions. We program our children to like such things. Need proof? Leave empty boxes, sticks, blocks, and wrapping paper in the room and watch the magic happen.

In this exercise, you need to find out your child's natural interests. This can be challenging when we are constantly distracted by shiny new objects that are designed to have a single use. A lip gloss making kit is designed only to make lip gloss. I am using this as an example to clarify what a single-use activity is.

In order to help you determine what your child really likes, as a visual (see what I'm doing here?), imagine yourself in a small cottage in the middle of nowhere with no wifi, or in a stalled car on the side of the road, with none of your child's favorite toys and no electronics. What will your child want to play with? How will he or she keep busy?

This visualization will help you determine, to the core, what your child likes. What naturally stimulates him or her without the material world's distractions. Will he or she revert to singing? Wiggle and dance? Want to explore the world around them?

Still not sure? That is OK. Test it out instead.

Go to the park or on a walk in your neighbourhood without any of the toys you usually bring (water, snacks, and other essentials are important - do not leave those out). What is your child drawn to? Does he or she react to sounds (birds, trucks, dogs)? Is he or she going straight for the sandbox, mud puddle, rolling around in the grass? Is he or she all about exploring the area, observing every little thing that shows up in the path? Or does he or she prefer to stay by your side, waiting for you to initiate play?

It is important to note here that this exercise will not work if you force play on your child or structure the playtime. Let your child go. You still need to supervise, but allow your child to roam freely and initiate the play. Many children are not taught or are not allowed to play freely, so it is possible that your child does not know what to do and how to play.

Do not be harsh on yourself or on your child if that is the case. This scenario is a perfect teachable moment to identify the changes you need to make in your parenting approach. If your child does not know how to play freely, then your parenting style is creating challenges for your child, preventing the development of decision-making, problem-solving, critical thinking, and creativity. Adjustments will need to be made. This does not mean that your parenting style is wrong. This will happen, the majority of the time, because we are doing everything we can to keep our children safe and happy.

If your child needs to be shown or encouraged to play freely, lead him or her to different areas and ask open-ended questions such as: "What is the first thing that you see here?" Play by incorporating all 5 senses (What do you smell? What do you see? What do you hear? How does that feel to the touch?) and you will soon see your child light up. Please make sure that the smelling, touching, and tasting parts are safe.

---

2. How does your child learn?

Does your child focus better with pictograms and other visual aids? Does your child automatically try to touch or taste everything he or she sees? Does sound or music stimulate your child? Does your child react to touch? Does he or she light up with different sounds?

You think your child is too young for you to answer these questions? That is OK. Try this.

Babies make different gurgling sounds and watch for reactions from the adults around them. Be sure to react when your baby makes noises and watch his or her reactions. Watch how they react when other adults interact with them.

Lightly massage your baby's legs or back and see how he or she will react. How does your baby behave when you are in full face-to-face interactions with him or her?

With older children (toddlers, preschoolers, or even older), watch if your child doodles or fidgets when you talk to him or her. Does your child hum, sing, or narrate stories while doing work, colouring, or playing?

These examples will help you determine what type of learner the child is. Remember that there is not one learning style that is better than another. It is not your child's learning style that will have him or her struggle in school. It is using the wrong teaching style that will cause your child to struggle. Once you know how your child learns, studying and homework will no longer be a struggle because you will know how to teach new concepts to your child.

It is important to note here that modifying the way we teach in a classroom to accommodate every learning style does not require more work from the teacher. It is unrealistic to expect teachers to teach their lessons six different ways in order to help six different learning styles. There is however a way to incorporate teaching tools and aids that will help each learning style simultaneously in one lesson plan. I will elaborate on that later on in the book.

---

3. How does your child communicate?

Children communicate through 100 languages, and only one of those 100 languages is spoken. Finding out how your child communicates goes beyond the words he or she uses. Whining, screaming, clicking, and tapping are all methods of communication. Are you paying attention to what your child is telling you non-verbally?

It can take up to 30 seconds for a young child (or a differently-abled child) to process the information they are given properly. This is the minimum time it will take for them to answer you. Generally speaking, your child's silence does not mean that he or she is ignoring you or disrespecting you. It means your child is computing and processing what you just told them.

Here is the best exercise to do in order to understand the seriousness of your child's silence and how you react to it. Ask yourself: "What time is it?" and count to 10 before you answer. Now ask the question again and count to 30. If you thought 10 seconds was a long time to wait, 30 seconds feels like an eternity!

Going back to the fact that it can take up to 30 seconds for a young child to process the words that were just spoken, you will now be able to see the number of times you stopped your child from communicating with you because you did not understand his or her silence properly.

Most adults will start talking again or asking other questions after a 3-second pause, then again, and again, and again. In the time it takes for you to give your child three to five other commands or follow up questions to the original one, he or she is finally ready to answer the first command. But now you have added another minute or two to your child's computing process. There is no way your child can go through with your expectations at this point. Without even knowing it, you have set your child up for complete failure in communication.

This fact also holds true for children learning more than one language at a time. We often think that they are simply not understanding the language we are communicating with. In reality, they are simply processing the verbal commands in not only one language, but in every other language they are introduced to.

How does your child communicate? Will he or she whine and scream to get your attention? Does your child throw tantrums when he or she does not get his or her way? Does your child use his or her hands to communicate? How about those eye rolls and sighs of disgust? These are all forms of communication from your child.

Knowing this now, how well are you actually listening to your child's way of communicating with you? Children observe what we do, not what we say. If you are not paying attention to the 100 different ways your child is communicating with you, you are teaching them not to pay attention to you when you are communicating with them.

---

4. What are your child's social interactions?

How does your child behave in a social setting? There are many different types of personalities, and ALL are absolutely marvelous. There are many kinds of tests you can do to identify your child's dominant personality traits. These tests are quite fun to do as a family to determine everyone's personality. These tests will also tell you how to speak to certain people and what their triggers are.

The Colors personality test and the Hats personality test are great to do with children. You can find free versions of these tests online. I encourage you to try them out. They are great activities to do between siblings or in a classroom. They sensitize everyone to other people's feelings and are a great way to encourage compassion and active listening.

Knowing your child's personality type will help you determine how your child will interact with the outside world. It will give you the upper hand on how to prepare your child for different types of social interactions and how to support them in recovering from stressful situations. Being armed with these resources will have a positive impact on your child's mental health. Do not skip this part.

It is important to note here that your child's true personality only comes out in free, unstructured play. Children put on masks when they are involved in structured play. They become who we expect them to be for the activity, so their true nature will not shine through.

5. Mirror, Mirror... What are you really teaching your child?

Every child learns by observing adults' actions. What are you transferring to the child that you are not even aware of? Do you put into practice the morals and the integrity you are teaching your children verbally?

It is important to note that we cannot be too hard on ourselves with this one. We all slip up at some point or another. We will all, at some point, tell our children to behave a certain way "because we said so." We will all, at some point, punish our kids for something that we do in front of them continuously.

The best way to set your child up for success is to start with listening to your expressions. What do you say when you are surprised? What do you say when you are overwhelmed? How do you refer to people when they do something that upsets you? How do you talk about the other parent when you are joking around? Your child is taking note of every word you say, even when you think they are not listening.

Pay attention to how you react to certain situations. Your child is soaking in all this new knowledge that your actions and reactions are teaching them. Your child does not listen to what you teach them; he or she imitates what you do. It is your duty as a parent to do the work and the healing necessary to make sure your words match your actions.

Feeling overwhelmed with all this information?

I realize that this exercise can feel overwhelming. Investing the time with these steps will help you become the ultimate supporter for your child. By knowing what your child needs at every stage of his or her development, you will be able to make the necessary decisions with confidence. You will also be able to stay the course with ease when outside influences try to make you question what is the best for your child.

The "Teacher's Corner" playlist on my YouTube channel has a series of videos in which I walk you through how to identify your child's play patterns and learning styles, as well as show you how to enhance their learning experiences with this information. Here is the link once again:

"You can learn many things from children. How much patience you have, for instance."

- Franklin P. Jones

CHAPTER 3:
CELEBRATING THE WINS

One of the things we hardly ever do as parents is to tap ourselves on the back when we have moments of awesomeness. We quickly cover them up with sarcastic remarks or brush them off, waiting for the bad moments to hit us again.

It is important at this point to focus on the fact that you are a phenomenal parent. Celebrate your moments of awesomeness! No one will do it for you so celebrate those wins every... single... time.

I have strategically chosen this topic for the third chapter to solidify in you the notion that you are a great parent, that you are doing the best you can with the resources that you have, and that, as long as you have your child's needs in mind when you are making your parenting decisions, you are doing an amazing job.

Now that you have identified your Core Values, that you know how you want to show up as a parent, and that you know how your child is showing up, it is time to shift your dynamic in a positive way. Celebrating yourself as a parent is not going to be an easy task. We are conditioned to judge parents harshly, criticizing everything they do and second-guessing their abilities.

You are a good parent

I have worked with thousands of parents in the span of my career, and I have not once met someone who wakes up in the morning asking themselves what they can specifically do that day to intentionally hurt their child.

As a parent, you need to acknowledge the fact that you do what you can, with what you have, at that particular moment. As long as you have the best intentions for your child at the time you make your decisions, then you have made the right decision. It is only once you know better that you can do better.

Start celebrating the micro-wins

Working the "confidence" muscle as a parent is not easy. Just like any new form of training, it gets better the more you practice. If you decide to train yourself to do 100 push-ups, you know you will not be able to do all 100 on the first try. You will start with one, maybe 2, maybe 5. But you know that if you keep going and stay consistent, you will reach the 100 push-ups goal.

The same goes for getting yourself to believe that you have great parenting skills. You need to start by celebrating the mini-wins, no matter how little they are. I am still surprised at how many times parents will ask me how little the wins need to be. My answer is always the same: "Very little." The kind of little that will be comparable to one push-up, not a full push-up, the one you do standing, pushing up against a wall!

You are working on the ability to recognize all the great things you do as a parent throughout the day, while being pulled in every direction with your other life's responsibilities.

Your mini-wins must be little enough that you are forced to pay close attention to the little ways you show up for your child.

Identifying the great milestones is easy, but they are often far apart and hard to achieve. Once you focus on your tiny moments of awesomeness, you will see that you are indeed rocking parenthood.

If you find yourself at a low point as a parent, celebrate the fact that you got yourself out of bed in the morning. If you were not able to get yourself out of bed, celebrate the fact that you were able to open your eyes for a minute. As a parent, you can understand that there are days when that will be a very difficult task to accomplish.

This may seem extreme, but that is how you will get to see that you are showing up as a parent the minute you open your eyes.

As you are working on solidifying your Core Values and integrating them into your life and as you are beginning to understand how your child learns and grows, start paying attention to the moments you are showing up exactly the way you want to show up.

Breaking it down to bite-size moments

Forget the big moments - those are easy to pinpoint. The big wins are also important, but, at this stage, you want to focus on the little things. I like to compare this to someone who is training for a marathon. The marathon itself is a great feat that will be celebrated with a bang. However, you will not get up one morning and finish a marathon in record-breaking time.

You will first need to convince yourself to get up and start running. Getting up is a win. Celebrate it.

You got dressed to go running... that is a win. Celebrate it.

You got your running shoes on... that is a win. Celebrate!

Once these celebrations begin to motivate you to keep pushing, then you can focus on celebrating the stretches, the interval training, the strength training, the healthy eating, and so on.

A person who makes the decision to run a marathon will have to fight with their mind to accomplish every one of those steps at some point in the training. Do not take any of these accomplishments for granted. They are important. If you skip them, you may not make it to the marathon.

I use this analogy often because parenting is very much a marathon. As a parent, train yourself to celebrate the little moments that lead up to the big accomplishments. Celebrate every day.

You opened your eyes... YAY! You are out of bed.... Amazing! You got the children out of bed... Congratulations! Your celebrations do not need to be elaborate. Smile, do a little happy dance, tap yourself on the back, whatever works for you.

What do your mini-wins look like? I'd love to hear about them! You are more than welcome to share them with me. I will gladly cheer you on throughout your parenting journey.

What your children see

I also recommend getting your children involved. Ask them to point out the moments you showed up as a great parent. They see you through a different lens. They will point out things you would not even think would be categorized as great parenting.

When I was working with a group in a transitional home for women who were victims of domestic violence, one of the ladies pointed out that it was her oldest son who helped her see how he needed her to show up for him and his siblings during their very difficult transition.

From the first day she entered the transitional home, she was focusing her time and energy on getting her reports done for the lawyers, getting used to some kind of routine in her new environment, healing from the physical and psychological wounds of the traumatic experiences, and playing the "everything is normal" game at work.

During this time, she was being quite hard on herself for being too tired to spend more time with her children. It was on one exhausting night, when she was doing dishes with her oldest son, thinking about the million and one things she needed to get done once the kids would be in bed, that her son told her the one thing she needed to hear.

As they were finishing up the dishes and wiping everything down, he said to her: "You know, Mommy, doing the dishes with you was fun. I like it when we get to spend some time together like this." She was stunned. In her mind, she was not doing anything right for her children. She was feeling guilty that, with everything else her children had to go through, she was forcing them to do house chores. But for her child, that was the quality time he needed.

Getting your children involved in pointing out the mini-wins will also get them to see how amazingly you show up for them. It will give them a head start on recognizing the merits of parents for when their turn comes. Look at how awesome you are as a parent... You are already teaching your children important life coping skills!

EXERCISE - A GREAT TOOL TO HELP YOU WORK THAT MUSCLE

Still not seeing what spurt of awesomeness you dished out today? You picked up this book... Celebrate!!! You made it to Chapter 3! Even better!!!! You are putting it into practice...AWESOME!!!!

It is by working with thousands of parents throughout my professional life that I realized that we are conditioned to think that parenting is meant to be hard. The media and social influences paint the parenting journey as a negative experience. Parenting was never meant to be hard.

It is easier to focus on what is going wrong when it comes to raising children. This is one challenge to working our "awesome parent" muscles. How can we see our mini-wins if we're only looking at our obstacles?

That is how my "Parenting With Gratitude" journal came to be. I was looking for an additional tool to help parents work that "awesome" muscle.

As a big thank you for supporting my work by reading this book, I am including a free digital copy of my "Parenting with Gratitude" Journal available on Amazon. You can download it instantly with the following link: https://beingconnected.ca/book

Want a hardcopy of the journal?
Here is where you can purchase it:
https://beingconnected.ca/journals

"Safety and security don't just happen. They are the result of collective consensus and public investment. We owe our children, the most vulnerable citizens in our society, a life free of violence and fear."

- **Nelson Mandela**

PART 2:
BUILDING UP YOUR VILLAGE

Parenting was never meant to be hard. Caring for a child was originally backed up by an entire family, community, and village. Everyone in direct or indirect contact with the child had responsibilities regarding that child. The parents were never left by themselves to care for their children.

It is only once we separated the parents from their communities that things started getting hard. Separating the parents and the child from their support system was a great way to gain power over people. Raising future generations responsible for making this world a better place is not something that can be done alone.

As people started adopting the "not my child, not my problem" philosophy, communities began to fall apart. Children were now being robbed of a life full of compassion, understanding, and, most importantly, a sense of safety and security.

We need to put the focus back on the fact that we are ALL on the same team. Now that we are connected to the entire world, our "village" has grown exponentially, giving us access to unlimited resources.

But having been torn away from a supportive community, how can we trust other people to care for our children the way they deserve to be cared for?

The next three chapters will help shed light on how to use learnings from Part 1 to build your own "village" that will support you in meeting all of your child's individual needs.

While writing this book, I have had the privilege of interviewing professionals and specialists who are what I consider important people in any community. You will find, at the end of each of the chapters, advice, tips, and quotes from these outstanding individuals.

Centuries ago, and even decades ago, parents did not get to choose their village. They had to work with the community they were born into. Now that the world has completely opened up to all of us, we have the privilege of customizing our own "village" to watch our children bloom. We can find the people we can trust to guide and assist our children in becoming outstanding world leaders.

It is now time to figure out exactly what your "village" will look like for you.

"Children are great imitators. So give them something great to imitate."

- **Anonymous**

CHAPTER 4:
GETTING CLEAR ON WHAT YOUR VILLAGE WILL LOOK LIKE

Raising a child was never meant to be hard because there was an entire village supporting the family. Everyone was bringing in their expertise, having the child's best interest at heart.

Having a well-balanced, well-developed, and well-centered child meant, for the entire village, that they would become citizens to support them later on in life. The children became the future for the people, the retirement, health, and insurance plans so to speak. By investing their time in helping each child shine, they were ensuring a safe and secure future for them.

When I first thought about writing this book, I was reluctant to use the "Village" analogy. I found it to be a cliché, with some negative undertones. Over the years, I've come to realize that this is indeed the perfect analogy when it comes to parenting.

From the moment you find out you are becoming a parent, you will feel alone. You take on this burden of becoming the Super Parent that our social norms have led us to internalize. The first thing we need to teach all new parents is that whatever they are feeling, whatever fears they have, whatever worry, whatever disappointment they live with, they are not alone.

The only way we come to see this is by reaching out to others, having conversations with other parents, seeking wisdom from those who have lived it first. The most important thing to remember is that we need to do all this without judgment.

That is the Village. Your support group that will keep you somewhat sane along the way. It is important to note before moving on that the Village I refer to here is not an actual, geographical village.

The Village I refer to is the one you will build, as a parent, with members that are there to add value to your life and your child's life. It is the Village you chose.

A Village where you, as a parent, get to be the mayor, the chief, and the decision-maker for the well-being of your family.

By working with thousands of families in a span of nearly two decades, I have found it very efficient to build up a village in three steps.

Step One: YOUR support

Keeping in mind that the child should be, and will always be, at the center of your decisions, you must first start building up your village with citizens who will support you. It is not a selfish act. You can only show up for your child as well as you show up for yourself.

By determining your Core Values and by getting clear on how you are going to show up for your child as a parent, you will get a clear indication of what and who you need in your life to reach that level of awesomeness. Take a good look at where you are now and where you want to be. Imagine how you want things to work for you. Then, looking from that end result, look at where you are currently, and backtrack the necessary steps to get to your end goal.

Self-care and self-love are necessities when it comes to parenting. You have an infinite number of services at your disposal to recharge your battery. You do not need to set an outstanding budget to pamper yourself; many of the things can be done from home or within your community.

Once you know what works for you to recharge and reset, find what you need to get it.

One of the biggest mistakes you can make with this step is to follow the masses or the trends. Remember your Core Values and where you need to redirect your energy. A full day at the spa once a week may not be for you. Some prefer gardening, exercising, reading a good book, hiding from their family. Some like to recharge with a group of friends; some need to go into hermit mode and isolate for a short period of time. Forget about what social media tells you about what self-care is supposed to look like. Do what works for you!

Many will want to share their opinions on how you should handle your self-care. Many will also make you feel like you are not a good parent for taking time for yourself, referring to the sacrifices they have made as "Super Parents." Do not lose yourself in this noise. As long as you are not neglecting your child or avoiding your parental responsibilities to care for yourself, you are perfectly fine doing what works for you.

There will be a period of trial and error while you try to find the right balance in your life. You may want to try new things and get out of your comfort zone to find the right fit for you. You may realize that those new things are not for you. You may also notice that what worked for you 5 years ago may no longer be working for you. It is perfectly normal.

As you evolve as a parent, your needs and interests will evolve as well. A good indication that your values need to be re-evaluated or that your decisions need to be adjusted is when your go-to for self-care no longer does it for you. You may find yourself dreading doing the things you used to love doing. That is why it is very important to build YOUR village, a support system that will answer to your individual needs at any stage of your life.

Step Two: Your child's needs

Knowing that most of the support for your child needs will be coming from you, you want to enrich your home environment with people who make life easier. This support system will help you with the things you are struggling with as a parent.

If you need to seek outside help to support your child, know that this does not make you an unfit parent. On the contrary, this makes you an awesome parent. You recognize that whatever area you lack, someone else can provide. By having found your Core Values and your child's real needs, you are now ready to find the people you can trust with these supporting tasks. If the person is not right for the job, something will feel off.

This spans from finding people you trust to care for your child when you need an evening off or fall ill and seeking experts that will adequately help your child following a diagnosis.

Parenting is difficult with what we categorize as a "healthy" child. It becomes exponentially more difficult once your child needs additional attention and care. This book does include help for parents of differently-abled children, but addressing the totality of needs for differently-abled children will require more than a chapter.

I will always strongly stand on the premise that children cannot all fit in the same box. Therefore, the support needed for one child will not be the same as another. I invite you to reach out to me or have a look at the resources at the end of this book.

I will also always stand on the fact that there is no such thing as a defective child. Every child is perfect exactly as he or she is. We, as adults, need to recognize this, even if we are not dealing with other people's children or have no children of our own. I will repeat this often... there is no such thing as a defective child. There is however, a defective System.

That being said, as a parent, if you realize you require outside support for your child's healthy development, know that there is nothing wrong in asking for help. It is also perfectly ok not to be ok. A diagnosis or a label put on your child is difficult to accept. We want the best for our children.

You need to remind yourself that outside help is available for you and your child. It is not there to make things more difficult. As a civilization that does not rely on a village, we tend to see outside support as negative, fearing that people will judge us as unfit parents or, worse still, manipulate our children and take our rights away as parents.

In my experience as a parent and as an educator, I can tell you that the people who are willing to help really want to help. But they can only go as far as you will allow them to go. One of the biggest mistakes parents make is hoping to pass on their problems to someone who has absolutely no legal rights with regards to the child. Your child is not their child; you still have to make the decisions and do the work.

Taking it beyond your immediate parenting needs

Parenting often focuses on meeting our child's direct physical, emotional, and developmental needs. There are many other important aspects we tend to overlook. Beyond the essentials, addressing financial stability, community support, and family entertainment also plays a vital role in nurturing a well-rounded, healthy family life.

Sometimes, building your Village means physically relocating to another village. For many, the realities of moving to another city, or even abroad, bring on a plethora of emotions about starting a new life in a strange world. In the whirlwind of researching homes to move into, schools that are suitable for children, and so on, many of us do not realize that we have unlimited access to people who have a full database with all this information: real estate agents.

We tend to think that their sole purpose is to help us sell and buy homes, but it goes much further than that. They have access to the amenities, transportation, cultural services, etc. When physically moving into a new village, real estate agents can become your "one stop shop" for all the information you need.

Beyond utilizing the extensive resources real estate agents offer to help navigate the physical aspects of a community, you should consider other key areas to support a well-rounded family life. Consulting with financial advisors can provide clarity and direction, helping to establish a secure and sustainable plan for your family's future.

At the same time, introducing your children to the Arts fosters creativity, enhances their cognitive and emotional development, and strengthens family bonds through shared cultural experiences.

Additionally, encouraging physical activity through organized sports such as dance or martial arts can provide numerous physical and emotional benefits, promoting discipline, teamwork, and resilience. By embracing these diverse opportunities, you create a dynamic environment that supports every aspect of your family's growth and well-being.

While writing this book, I have had the privilege of interviewing amazing people in various fields who have shown me how their expertise really does help in building communities. You will find their thoughts and experiences on this subject at the end of this chapter.

Step Three: Finding the support your child will need in the outside world

This primarily means at school first. As parents, we often make the mistake to think that the schools have everything covered. That is where we will also forget that the teachers can only go as far as it is legally possible for them. Only you can make the calls on how to handle your child's academic success.

This has the potential to create friction between parents and schools, leading to both parties being forced to get on the defensive, everyone pointing the finger at everyone else and completely forgetting about the child in the process.

Parents are the first educators of their children. They hold vital information that will help teachers and educators support their children and lead them to success. If parents refuse to share this information for fear of being judged by the school, then the child will not be properly supported at school.

It is the schools' duty to create an environment where parents feel safe to divulge personal and difficult information about their child. Parents and teachers must work together. They must work as a team to make a positive change and re-establish trust.

Dismantling an important support system for the sole purpose of proving who is right is setting our children up for failure. Knowing this, why are we still fighting against our own team? Why has the child, the only thing that matters, been taken out of the equation when it comes to raising and educating children?

Teachers are spread thin and budgets are running on less than bare minimum. Your child's specific needs may not be met at school for the simple reason that the school is not informed of those specific needs. A big mistake we make as parents is to keep our child's individual needs a secret for fear of being judged or for fear that our child will be labeled.

We all understand how agonizing it is to have a child targeted as "different." By getting both the parents and the schools to focus on the fact that they are on the same team and working for the same goal, this challenge can be easily remedied.

I find it important here to clarify that the common goal is the child's healthy development. There is a need to put our ego and our pride aside when it comes to raising and educating children. It has nothing to do with us. It will never have anything to do with us.

It is all about the child. It was always about the child. It will always be about the child.

When it comes to the outside world that is not school-related, you will also need to look at what your child needs for their physical development (do you need to look at activities in your community?), their socio-emotional development (what does your child need to develop healthy relationships outside of the home?), and their cognitive development (will they need more support for language skills and other academic skills?).

Let us not forget that free, unstructured play is the only way children learn. Where, when, and how can your child have access to safe and healthy environments where they can explore their world freely?

What next?

Once you have outlined what your Village needs to look like, it is time to start building it. Do the research and find the people who will work well with you, but most importantly, will work well with your child. There may be some trial and error at first. Just remember that your Core Values and your child's real needs will help you find the right "citizens" for your Village.

EXERCISE - THE 3 STEPS OF SKETCHING OUT YOUR VILLAGE

---

1. Make a list of the support YOU need to show up fully as a parent. Find what will help you recharge your battery in the most realistic way. Now make a list of the people around you (family, friends, colleagues, etc.) who genuinely offer you that support.

    Start decluttering the people you interact with regularly (family, friends, social circles). Which individuals drain you? Which ones uplift you?

2. Make a list of the types of support your child needs that you are struggling to provide. Start researching which individuals could provide this support. Ask your child's school, your public library, and your community center for resources.

3. Make a list of the support your child will need for his or her school, sports club, etc. Find the groups that will be able to help your child feel safe in the outside world.

With these 3 steps, you will have a better picture of what and who you need in your Village. Give yourself time to find the right individuals. Ask for second opinions when you are not convinced the first person has given you accurate information.

The most important part, once you start building your Village, is to be straightforward with the people you are looking to for support. The right people will not have any issues with helping you and your child.

Checking in on the dynamic of your Village regularly will be necessary to make sure that everything still works. As your child gets older and as life experiences change, so will the support you need. It will be necessary to update the citizens of your Village along the way.

The next chapter will help you find the right approach to building your Village.

But first, here are the advice and tips given by the extraordinary people I have interviewed for this book.

The Self-Care Connection: Experts sharing the power of nurturing yourself

There are loads of clinical and medical information about the benefits of taking care of yourself as a parent. Having a more "hands-on" approach to my research, I thought it would be important to go straight to the source. I have had the pleasure of interviewing amazing people who run their businesses solely on self-care. Who better than to hear from the people who see, first hand, the transformation of people after a session at their spa? Here are some of their incredible observations.

Rachelle McMahon, from Spa Passion by Rachelle (spapassionbyrachelle.com) describes the transformation she sees in her clients from before and after one of the soul-nourishing treatments she offers:

"They come in stressed, tired, and feeling truly disconnected. During the treatment, I can feel their energy change. They leave feeling lighter and calmer, with a deep sense of nourishment, not only from their skin, but from the inside out. They feel soulfully nourished, valued, heard, and cared for. We all need to be soulfully nourished. That is so important."

Donna Holtom from Hotz Spa in Nature (holtzspa.com) gives great insight on how to change our mindset about self-care:

"Turn away from the guilt and have a good look at yourself. Change the word guilt to responsibility. It is our responsibility to take care of ourselves, to be better human beings. Self-care is not just for the elite anymore. The younger people understand this much better."

Anindya (Andy) and Indrani from York Street Spa (yorkstreetspa.com) took it even further, mentioning how involving your children in the process as they get older not only creates solid bonds between parent and child but also sets a great example to the children on developing this great habit. They shared their philosophy on the importance of self-care:

"They [the clients] get a boost in confidence and a boost on how to deal with difficult situations. They have a feeling that they can go and face the world with more confidence. That I think is the transformation that I see in the clients that come in. Don't feel shy or guilty. This Me Time, you need everyday in different ways.Coming to the Spa is your Me Time. That really helps the whole family. Me Time is so

important. In modern day time, we go through so much stress. The little bit of Me Time is very helpful not only for us but for society at large.

We often associate self-care to spa treatments but it goes beyond that. Imagine yourself coming home from a stressful day, to a clean house! Keeping a clean home plays a large role in our stress level. We often dismiss the idea of getting someone to maintain our homes for us, not liking the idea of having strangers literally going through our dirty laundry. This concept is widely misunderstood and worth investing into.

Stephanie Applejohn from Merry Maids of Ottawa (merrymaidsottawa.ca) shares recommendations on how to but your worries to rest and take a large burden off your hands:

"It's OK to ask for help. Life is too short. You have to spend time with family and friends, and people that you care and love the most. If you feel that you are not spending enough time, then you need to re-analyze what you can get help with. People spend 4 hours/week cleaning. Those 6 hours could be spent making memories with your friends and family."

Freeing your time from house work has such a positive impact on a person that some businesses incorporate it into their business model. A great cosmetic company, renowned worldwide, highly recommends that once their representatives become team leaders, that they invest in housekeeping and other home services. The reasoning behind this is that the time spent cleaning and maintaining their house could be spent on building their business and making memories with their families.

Reflection Question:

I wanted to mention that here since self-care can come in multiple forms. What other types of self-care could you and your family benefit from?

I could write a whole other book on self-care practices alone! It is time to move you now towards the actual physical Village. The next section will walk you through it.

The Community Connection: Experts sharing a broader impact in your neighbourhood

1. **Neighbourhood, Amenities, Commute, Schools, and so much more:**

Building your village can be both literal and metaphorical, especially when moving abroad and starting fresh in a new environment. Real estate agents, often seen as solely facilitating property transactions, actually hold the key to much more - they are your gateway to local amenities, transportation, cultural services, and more. Through my interviews with exceptional real estate professionals, I have discovered how their expertise plays a crucial role in building and nurturing communities. Here is what they had to say about how their work goes beyond the sale.

While writing this book, I have had the privilege to talk to **Anna Alemi** (annaalemi.com), a Real Estate Broker, who devotes a lot of her time helping new families settle into Ottawa, Canada by providing valuable information that newcomers may not even consider when moving to a new country:

"When you are looking from the outside, everybody looks the same to you. One of the most important things is to get out there and to know that there are different services available, different types of people available to you to cater to your needs, and not one person necessarily matches your needs. In Canada, that's the beauty of it, you have a nice, diverse type of people that are available to you and that speak to you."

Kiril Peev (kirilpeev.com), from Kiril Peev Real Estate, adds interesting insight on the important role a real estate agent can play for families who are relocating and want to make sure they choose the right community for their family:

"In North America, we tend to be overprotective of our kids. Whereas other cultures kind of have a more intuitive trust that things are going to work out. I really try to understand the type of lifestyle they live and then match the home to their lifestyle. But also, what are things that they are overlooking, will things change in 10 years? Details matter."

A.J. Plant (www.ajplant.com), Broker and Regional Owner of EXIT Realty Eastern Ontario, takes the subject further by revealing the unadvertised work that most real estate agents pour back into the communities. Here is what he shared with me:

"Many agents take part of their commission and put it back in the community by sponsoring and coaching teams, playing an active part in the School Boards, and even becoming politicians in their communities. They also create jobs through assistants for their agents, inspectors, photographers, printers, etc.

We are actively involved in shaping that community and it is a duty to give back through running an empathy-based business."

I have to be honest that when I first thought of bringing in the real estate side of a Village, I was not sure where it would go. It became clear to me that the message that had to come out of these incredible and insightful conversations with these amazing individuals is that you have choices, and once you are clear on what you and your family needs, you will find the community that will understand and support your needs.

Buying a home may not be a reality for you. Know that the limitless resources that real estate agents have are not limited to buying and selling customers.

2. Budget, Finances, College Funds, Retirement, and so much more:

Financial troubles are a significant source of stress for parents and can deeply affect how they engage with their child. While seeking financial advice is often viewed negatively, taking control of one's financial situation can be an empowering step that not only reduces stress but also sets a positive example for a child's future financial freedom. By addressing these challenges proactively, parents can create a more stable and nurturing environment for their family.

This is why I thought it would be important to interview a few professionals in the finance world to shed some light on a topic that is still quite taboo for most. Here is the wisdom they shared with me:

Andrew W. Bradley (andrewwbradley.ca), shares the transformation he sees in people from how they feel about their current finances to after their financial plan is implemented:

"Most people I work with, it keeps them up at night, they worry about it. All this thinking weighs on them. So just to get that weight off their shoulders when they have it taken care of, they can exhale, and breathe, and know that they are OK."

Ayana Forward (ayanaforward.ca), from Retirement in View, has a unique approach to finances and walks her clients through a realistic understanding of financial independence:

"No one likes to budget. Budgeting is like a diet. I know I should be doing it, but it is not the be-all and end-all. I point out your strengths, your weaknesses, what you are missing, and then how to not just look at it from a financial perspective, but a lifestyle as well."

Finances are, by far, a major source of stress for parents. Taking that into consideration and getting a sense of the guidance you need in that area will help you find the key players of your Village to lead you to financial stability.

This should not be as taboo of a subject as it has been for generations. Financial advisors and planners are also bound by confidentiality clauses, making it even more reassuring when taking the first steps to implement a financial plan that will work in your favour.

3. Arts in the Community:

Engaging in community arts activities offers tremendous benefits for a child's development, fostering creativity, emotional growth, and cognitive skills. At the same time, these shared experiences can enhance family bonds and create meaningful quality time together. Exploring the arts together helps build a more connected and enriched family life.

Arts is no longer for the elite only. You can access various forms of the Arts in any community, with many of these activities being accessible at no cost.

I have had the privilege of interviewing two amazing people who are very active in the world of the Arts. Here is what they had to share:

Anik Bouvrette, from Tara Luz Danse (taraluzdanse. ca), shares her view on the benefits of bringing access to the Arts to communities who do not readily have access to it. This quote has been translated from our French interview:

"It is a human right! We must realize that access to the Arts brings wonder, no matter the age. For children, it fosters great curiosity, openness, and a thirst for learning."

Jahn Fawcett, who oversees Community Building Through Art at the Shenkman Art Center, has offered first-hand wisdom about the developmental benefits of introducing the Arts to children:

"For some kids that do not see it right away, it gives them exposure and a basic understanding that helps them consider the same problem from a different perspective. And for those kids where Art is a big part of the way they think and interact with the world, it is just going to set them free."

Jahn started off the interview by saying something that I think sums up this section very well:

"Don't be afraid, just dive in and try something. Increasingly, we are seeing the barriers of High Art being broken down. It is no longer a place for the few. From adult colouring books to repair sewing parties, there's just a way to integrate art into everyday life. Just make something."

4. Physical activity that can help self-regulate:

Certain physical activities not only promote a child's overall physical health but also play a vital role in their socio-emotional development and self-regulation.

Sports like martial arts, dance, and team-based games can be particularly beneficial for children facing various challenges, providing them with structure, confidence, and a healthy outlet for their emotions.

Engaging in these activities can help children build resilience, discipline, and a strong sense of self. While writing this book, I have had the opportunity to interview many great experts in these various fields. Here is what they shared with me:

Ben Clarke, from Douvris Martial Arts (orleans.douvris. com), has a fresh point of view on the impact martial arts have on a child's self-esteem and confidence. Opening up his martial arts school at the age of 18, he shares powerful insights on his experience:

"I was shy as a kid. Karate helped me with my confidence. It helped me meet different friends outside of school. Becoming a teacher at 14 also helped with my shyness. I noticed I handled issues differently from my friends. Seeing them going to the mall while I was training, I noticed a difference in maturity level. My self-confidence and focus were high.

My parents say it was the best $5 they ever spent".

Kailena Van de Nes, from Live Well With KV (livewellwithkv.com), offers a great perspective as owner of a dance studio:

"The fundamental importance for any kid who wants to pursue anything, whether it's dancing or underwater basket weaving, starts with the intrinsic desire to learn more and to master that skill. Therefore, if your child shows an interest in a specific sport or art, let them explore it as much as possible. The more time and energy they dedicate to their interest, essentially the better they should become. Of course, this is not the case for all children. Some are naturally more artistic, or more athletic. This is why exploring a variety of interests will help your child find something they are passionate about.

Another very important skill to teach your child as young as possible, as they seek out their passions in life, is how to be autonomous. When it comes to accomplishments, rewards, and achievements, learning autonomy is such an important life skill. When children seek out validation for all of their achievements, it will be tougher to build self-motivation down the line. Teaching them to be proud of their own accomplishments can help avoid the constant comparisons to peers that naturally can happen in any environment."

———————————————————————

Scott Blandford, from West-End Jiu-Jitsu (westendjiujitsu. com), offers a much different view of the benefits of the martial arts. Serving as a police officer, he directed most of his dojo's programs to help at-risk youth and young adults. Here is what he shared with me regarding setting your child up for success in life:

"Street-proof them. No bubbles! Burst that bubble. Educate them on bullying behaviours and how to recognize them".

Darryl D'Amico, from Ottawa Jeet Kune Do (ottawajkd. com), offers very sage insight from having worked with children for many years:

"I think every kid has the potential to be what they want to be but at a young age (6+ years), they don't know what that is. I think some parents need to realize that and understand that their son or daughter has this great potential. What we try to do is bring that out of those kids."

There are so many more people, from many more fields, that I could have interviewed. I believe and hope that this section has helped you see just how big you can grow your village to be.

The third part of building your Village is to provide the support your child needs for the outside world. The next section provides great resources to help you connect with the right people.

The Guiding Hands Connection: Trusted Advice for Raising Resilient Children

In this section, you will hear from leading specialists such as speech therapists, autism mentors, tutors, and so many more who offer invaluable insights to help your child thrive. Their expert advice and personal experiences will empower you with the knowledge and confidence to support your child's unique needs and foster their growth. Trusting the professionals you may need to bring on board within your Village can make a significant difference in your child's journey to success.

Scott Murray, who was Headmaster at a prestigious school in Brockville, Ontario at the time of the interview, offered insight on how the way we handle Education needs to change in order to properly prepare our children to become the future world leaders. It was rather refreshing to be able to converse with someone that shared the same views on Education as me:

"The World is getting smaller and smaller by the day. This generation of children is going to work in multicultural places, they are going to connect far more than even my generation and the generation after me. It's going to be the

reality of the World, they are going to have to work and deal with people from other cultures.

The more schools can make that part of their curriculum, the better everybody is going to be in the end. It should not be seen as a challenge; it should simply be what we do".

Krupa Patel, a private tutor in the Ottawa region, shares how difficult it is for parents to see that their child could be struggling with certain subjects at school. The communication with the school can also make that even more difficult. Here is her advice for parents on how to approach their worries:

"Be in close touch with your kid. For some kids, math is just not their subject. There is nothing wrong with getting a tutor for your 5-year-old. The early years are the key to making sure we are bridging those learning gaps".

Staying true to myself and choosing a more unconventional approach to building my Village, I have had the chance to interview a great family in which the mother is an Early Childhood Educator and the father is a skilled woodworker. Together, they make an incredible team for creating educational toys for children. Here is what **Brian and Jessica** from Cogneato Toy Co shared on the importance of getting the proper toys and multi-purpose/multi-use learning materials for your child's development:

"Having child-led learning and having the different materials to use the way that they want to promote hand-eye coordination, creativity, imagination, as well as cognitive and problem-solving skills."

Gail Palmer MSW, RMFT, one of the founders of the Ottawa Couple and Family Institute and from the Ottawa EFT Centre (ottawaeftcentre.com) offers exceptional insight on the importance of a strong family bond to foster a child's resilience:

"Empathize with your child first before jumping to correction first. This makes kids feel safe, understood, and shows that parents have confidence in their kids. Try to meet your kid halfway if possible, be curious about their behaviour".

Sabrina McTaggart, a career coach for young adults (sabrinamctaggart.com), gives us a broader view of how we can support our children well into the adult years:

"Our teenagers will often appear to be pushing us away (I'm not listening to you, You don't know anything), but it is important for parents to remember they are listening, they are watching, and they are soaking up everything their parents say."

As an Occupational Therapist, **Meghan Topolnisky** B.A, MScOT Reg., founder of Expanding Horizons (expandinghorizonsot.com), offers great advice for parents who begin the process of getting additional support for their child:

"Being a parent is difficult. Don't be hard on yourself on the lower days. It is consistency over time that creates success. Every parent has their limitations. As parents, we need to ask ourselves: what can I do to help my child? That is why we have a team for the hard days. Ask for help".

John Anderson, from Spectrum Insights (spectruminsights.ca), devotes his time in helping teenagers and young adults on the autism spectrum maintain regular exposure to the outside world. His view on the difficulties individuals face when they no longer have access to additional support after reaching the age of adulthood is quite eye-opening:

"The kids have a hard time transferring the skills they have learned 1 on 1. They need somebody to physically be there to remind them what to say and what to do in a social scenario. They have to get additional support to remind them how to manage sensory issues out there. It can be as easy as phoning a friend.

Having someone interacting with the child helps show them what positive peer-to-peer interactions look like."

As a speech therapist, **Lauren Barlow** (ottawaspeechtherapist.ca), explains the importance of seeking support early on:

"If you are not starting off early on, you're throwing your kid into a situation where they don't know how to tune into their environment.

A situation no parent wants their child to have to face alone."

Mme. Amy (Amy Warr), from 1 2 3 Petits Pas (123petitspas.com), shows an incredibly positive side of introducing your child to a new language and the beautiful bond you can forge by learning along with them:

"Kids don't need organized learning. They soak it all in so don't worry about mistakes. What a great opportunity to start from zero. Then there is no pressure. They can't judge you, you're learning alongside your child."

Christine L'Abbé, founder of The Conscious Practitioner and host of the podcast Evolving Together: Beyond the Diagnosis, Into a New Realm of Possibilities, offers deeply compassionate support for parents of children navigating neurodiversity and complex health needs. With both personal insight from her journey with her daughter Gabi, who has Rett syndrome, and her professional expertise as a Conscious Parenting Coach and Pediatric Anat Baniel Method® NeuroMovement® Practitioner, Christine has cultivated a nurturing community where parents find connection, hope, and empowerment. During our conversation, Christine highlighted the importance of parents prioritizing their own healing to order to truly support their children:

"Your child is deeply attuned to your inner world. They feel your energy—whether it's fear, judgment, or uncertainty— and mirror it in their own experience. When you choose to heal and nurture yourself, you shift the entire dynamic. You create a safe, loving space where your child can unfold into their highest expression, supported by the unwavering energy of your presence."

I hope this section was helpful in expanding your vision of your Village. I encourage you to look even further to make this parenting journey even more successful for you and your family.

"Children have never been very good at listening to their elders, but they have never failed to imitate them."

- **James Baldwin**

CHAPTER 5:
GETTING EVERYONE
ON THE SAME PAGE

The next step on this journey is to openly and clearly communicate what is required of your Village.

Everyone will have a specific role in your child's life. Like any city or organization is run, everyone in your Village needs to be clear on their roles and functions.

You, as the parent, need to communicate these expectations clearly from the beginning. Many will try to convince you that their way of thinking is best. When this happens, remember that most of them will really think they are helping you by voicing their opinions.

Going by your values and your child's needs, you will know whether or not their suggestions and recommendations are a right fit. Communication is key. Thank them for their advice; some days their thoughts will really help you. Challenges and unnecessary drama within a Village stems from the adults taking on their functions in a place of ego and pride. Remember that you are the mayor, the chief, the sheriff, and the elder of your Village. It will be up to you to get everyone to put the focus back on what matters... your child.

It is important that this Village must not become a dictatorship. Your child must be in a safe and nurturing community. Every person in it must be the warm and wonderful human being they are. The harmony between everyone involved will become the model your child will be looking for once in adulthood.

Too many times when working in daycares did I find myself stuck, unable to help a child because the parents did not want to share the necessary information. The message here will come across as harsh for some of you. If you choose not to share important information on your child's specific needs, then you need to accept that you are responsible for teachers, educators, and childcare providers not being able to support your child. They can only work with what you give them access to.

All information is helpful. I am not only speaking of special needs here. Basic information such as what comforts your child when he or she is feeling sad, frightened, or unwell? What scares him or her? What do you call their favorite teddy bear or toy? Do Grandma and Grandpa have special names?

Most schools and daycare centers ask these questions during registration. Do not skip these questions.

The impact of working against each other

All of these details will help your child feel heard and safe in the presence of people who show up in his or her life. This makes a tremendous difference in your child's life. As an educator, if you feel a resistance from the parents to share crucial information about their child's needs, it is your duty to create an environment where the parents will feel safe to share this information with you. You must make them feel that you are there to help them, that you are on the same team.

When dealing with children who require additional assistance, it is imperative to share this information with the Village that is affected by it. The harsh reality here is that, if you choose not to tell the key players in your child's outside world, such as the school or the child care provider, that your child has specific challenges that require additional resources, this decision will hurt your child in the long run as you are hindering these key players to adjust the way they show up for your child.

If you do not share this important information with your child's school, for example, the teachers and educators can only work at making your child fit into a box that he or she cannot fit into.

Also, it is important to mention that teachers and educators are trained to observe certain behaviours in your child that may require some attention. It is possible that someone approaches you to talk about some concerns regarding your child's behaviour. Sometimes, this will catch you off guard because your child may not display that kind of behaviour at home.

This does not mean that the school, daycare provider, or sports center are teaching your child this behaviour. As your child gets more exposure to the outside world, they will be faced with situations and emotions they have not yet experienced. This can trigger behaviours they have never displayed before.

By working as a team with the people who tend to your child when they are in the outside world, those behaviours will quickly be changed to allow your child to experience more positive interactions with their new environments.

Contesting the observations given to you and playing the blame game on who is responsible for these new behaviours will only create greater challenges for your child. Allow yourself to take on this new information, sort through what was given to you, and then make a suitable decision for your child.

I can tell you from experience that you will not be protecting your child from being labeled as being different by ignoring the issue. Teachers and educators are trained to notice the red flags in a child's development. They will know you are withholding important information and will be able to adjust to the best of their abilities. But as long as you do not give further information, they must follow the regular protocol for managing your child's behaviour. This protocol however, may not be suitable for your child's specific needs.

Your child will not know that he or she is struggling because of the information you are withholding or refusing to accept, leading them to believe that they are a "difficult" unworthy child and not knowing why.

As I mentioned in Chapter 3, I have never met a parent who wakes up in the morning wondering how they can torture their child. I can also tell you that I have never met a teacher who wakes up in the morning making it their mission to make your child miserable. We are all on the same team.

Opening the line of safe communication

Communication is important for the well-being of your child. Here is the information I recommend you share for your child to bloom in a positive and successful way:

- **Specific learning needs, learning styles, and personality traits:** This saves time for educators and teachers to have to figure it all out through trial and error. They have many more children they need to get to know as well. This establishes a safe and trusting learning environment much earlier for your child.

- **Your expectations on how things will be handled with your child:** It is within your rights to have your values respected as a parent. This information can be expressed in a respectful way, showing your willingness to keep communication open for the well-being of your child.

- **How to communicate with you:** Do you prefer people to reach you via a phone call or an email? What constitutes an emergency for you? Is there a preferred sequence of people to call first? This will reassure your support system that you are open and willing to work as a team for the sake of your child. Keep in mind that many are required by law to contact you regarding certain issues with your child, even if you do not consider those issues as emergencies.

I would take it one step further and ask everyone involved in your support system to specify their preferred way of communication. Are your child's teachers required to communicate through email or a specified parent-teacher group? What is the line of hierarchy to follow when having to deal with specific issues? By taking this extra step, all parties ensure a smooth partnership in helping the child reach his or her full potential.

By setting everything down from day one, everyone will know what their role is with regards to your child. It also holds everyone accountable if they choose not to follow through with their responsibilities.

The importance of updating the plan regularly

Once the foundation is laid down, if there is any resistance or discrepancy with the support provided for your child, it will be easier to identify the area that needs clarification or additional support.

Your child's needs will change as they grow, which will require you to review what is needed in your Village. A review of your support plan is also required after major changes or events, such as a change in teachers or school, the death of a loved family member, a divorce, a move, etc.

During these events, your child's insecurities and traumas will not necessarily be obvious. Keep your child's 100 languages in mind. Their grief, anxiety, and fears will more often than not be non-verbal. Do not take for granted that everyone will automatically know your child's specific needs.

Be sure to share the new information with everyone involved. Some individuals are not able to share the information you provide them due to confidentiality laws. And some individuals do not require this new information either. When I mention that your Village needs to be in the know, I do not mean that you need to have a "Town Hall" meeting with everyone.

Some conversations will be difficult. Every parent will, at some point, have an unpleasant discussion with a family member, a teacher, or a coach. Remember that the only thing that matters is your child, and every other child involved. Remember also that everyone is on the same team.

Make it clear when you need to talk to someone about your child that you are not questioning their abilities and their integrity. Set the intention that you are meeting to collaborate together in finding a solution to help your child before the meeting takes place so everyone is on the same page.

If the conversation turns to a blame game, end it. You are wasting your time and you are creating a toxic environment for your child. Keep it constructive and keep it respectful. We are all working for the child's well-being.

"Even if people are still very young, they shouldn't be prevented from saying what they think."

- Anne Frank

CHAPTER 6:
CHECKING IN WITH THE BOSS

As we navigated through the heavy work required from the previous chapters, we now need to put the focus back on what really matters... the child.

You have identified your Core Values, you know how you want to show up as a parent, you know your child and can identify your child's needs, you know where you need assistance, and you are finally beginning to build your true Village. The biggest mistake to make here is to forget to check in with your child to make sure that this is all working right.

As adults, we are quick to make assumptions about what we think our child needs. As teachers, we are quick to make assumptions about how a child needs to learn. We must remember that, in fact, the child is the only one who can tell us if everything is in working order.

A great teacher and mentor of mine, Marisa Peer, often says that our children come through us, not from us. We often claim our children as our property, our "mini-mes," when in fact, they are their own individuals who need to become who they are meant to be.

Respecting our child as an individual

We have to redirect our thought process in order to understand that our role in our children's lives is to support them through their development from infancy to adulthood. We have to make sure that what we do for them is for their benefit, not ours.

This means that the decisions we make and the plans we draw up to support them need to benefit them. There is no cookie-cutter way of raising a child; everyone is a unique individual. What works for one child will not work for another.

Once you have determined the support you need to raise a healthy, well-rounded child, you need to make sure that it works for your child. It is important to get your child age-appropriately involved throughout the process and check in on how they are feeling about the whole experience. Your child needs to feel safe in his or her Village.

Children need to know that they matter and that they add just as much value to the Village as the Village does to them. Talk to your child regularly about the changes that will happen. Seek out their opinion about the people who are supporting them and the work they are doing to help them. Sometimes your child will communicate this non-verbally so pay attention.

It is important to mention that this is not a consultation with your child where they get to make the decision. This is an opportunity to make the necessary changes as your child grows and matures.

A great example for this last statement is when your child reaches the age at which they can be home by themselves. An after school program may no longer be needed at that point. Would a "Safety at home" course be beneficial for your child to help them with that transition?

This is how tuning in with "the boss" will help you make informed decisions on the next steps to have in place for your child.

How to know if it works

Check in on your child to see if he or she feels comfortable with the plan. Be on the lookout for positive results.

If your child is motivated and illuminated, then you are on the right track. Open that line of communication with your child to see which areas need improvements and which ones need adjustments as your child grows and matures. Continue to keep the lines of communication open with everyone involved to make sure the Village is still on the same page. This may sound overwhelming at first, but once the Village is operational, things will get easier very quickly.

When you compare the time you spend worrying about the well-being of your child, wondering if he or she is safe at school, if you are going to get a call from the school, or if you are doing enough, versus the time it takes to send a quick note to a teacher or a specialist, you will notice that keeping the communication line open is a worthwhile investment.

It is all in your perspective. Where do you wish to spend your energy? In a positive, constructive environment? Or in an overwhelming, negative one? The choice is yours.

As you work towards showing up the way you want to show up as a parent, to separate your own personal needs from your child's actual needs, and finding the individuals you need to build a solid and safe Village for your child, you will need to learn how to troubleshoot when life throws you a curveball. You will need to know how to see the bigger picture so you are leading your child to a successful and fulfilling life.

It is now time to make sure you will keep moving forward.

"Children are likely to live up to
what you believe of them."

- **Lady Bird Johnson**

PART 3:
SETTING YOUR CHILD UP FOR SUCCESS

This last section of the book is designed to allow you to move forward from here, with all the work you have done so far.

You have determined your values and know how to show up as a parent. You know your child and are able to identify what help is needed. Finally, you now have the knowledge and the tools needed to build your Village accordingly. Does this sound like the answer to all your problems? Does it sound too good to be true?

The truth is, it is too good to be true. In a perfect world, your work would be done here and all would be smooth sailing from now on. Like I have mentioned in the previous chapters of this book, there is no cookie-cutter formula to solve all of our parenting challenges.

I cannot, with a clear conscience, tell you that if you follow this book to the letter, you will no longer have problems raising your child. That is a utopian ideal I cannot sell you.

There is no absolute solution for a particular problem because children are not all the same, parents are not all the same, and educators are not all the same. Even if you are dealing with the same concern or issue with several children, the outcome would differ because every situation and every family is unique.

It would be irresponsible for anyone to claim that they have found the miracle formula to raising healthy children. You will not find in this book a cure-all for raising a child with particular needs.

It is impossible to identify every situation that needs to be resolved because they are ever-changing and never-ending. Books that were written on particular issues need to be continuously updated because our children and our world are constantly changing and evolving.

This is why the next three chapters are devoted to helping you troubleshoot your plan when life throws you a curveball and making sure that, no matter what the setbacks will be, you will make the proper decisions to keep moving your child forward so that he or she can surpass you in life.

It is now time to help you stay on track when people and events will potentially try to make you lose your focus.

"There can be no keener revelation of a society's soul than the way in which it treats its children."

- Nelson Mandela

CHAPTER 7:
WHO, WHAT, WHEN, AND WHERE IS THE PROBLEM?

As mentioned in the introduction to Part 3, it would be irresponsible of me to sell you on the idea that, having completed the exercises in the last six chapters, your work is now complete. That is not the reality of parenting.

What I can do, however, is give you a process to follow, a guideline so to speak, that works for any situation life will throw at you. Following this process will help you reach an acceptable solution to help everyone involved in a problem relating to your child. All you will need to do is add the necessary components to your particular situation and customize the process to your particular issue.

The adaptable process

This process will work for any issue, spanning from trying to get your child to clean up his or her room to coming up with an action plan with your child's school to address recent violent outbursts.

How do you solve a problem that keeps recurring but is somehow different every time? What worked the first time will not necessarily work the second time. What works for one child will not necessarily work for another. That is why it is impossible to give you a cure-all answer moving forward. With the tools and resources you are given in this book, you will be able to customize this process to your specific needs, at any particular time.

The great thing about this process is that it is transferable to any area of life, not only parenting challenges. It will also work with your professional life, your friendships, and your relationships.

Here is the process:

In order to address the real issue and find the right solution or plan to remedy the problem, you must find the answers to the following questions:

- What is the real problem (the root cause of the problem)?

- Why is it a problem?

- Who has the problem?

- When and where is it a problem?

- Is everyone involved working to solve the same problem?

- Is the child included in the solution to the problem?

The last two points are the game changers in this process. It can be easy to determine the problem, who has it, why, when, and where it happens. But what then? The last two points are what helps us put it all together for an effective solution.

This process is another muscle to work. It will take time to be comfortable with it. Once you get the hang of it, I assure you that you will know how to adapt it to find solutions to any situation, whether they are related to your child or your own personal experiences.

Now let's get into the meat of it.

Identifying the root cause of the problem

The one thing you must remember through this whole process is that there is only one constant in this formula. That constant is that all issues pertaining to raising children stem from a problem.

Sounds simple enough, but what is the actual problem you are trying to solve? What is the true cause of the problem? Are you working on resolving the root cause of the problem or simply a side effect of the real problem?

Whatever the answers to these questions are, your real challenge in this process is to figure out whether everyone involved in solving the problem is working on solving the same problem.

Let me explain...

What is the problem? Sounds like a simple question to answer. However, once you meet with the people involved in the problem, you must pay attention to what that problem represents for each individual. Not everyone is experiencing the problem in the same way. If the problem is not clearly defined by every person involved and the intention of the solution is not established by everyone involved, it will become a whole other problem.

> *What is the problem?*
> *The biggest mistake you will make here, and the only reason why the process will not work, is by forgetting to look at the problem from every angle.*

In this chapter, I will give you a step-by-step guide to finding the real problem and thus finding an effective solution to a very difficult situation you may encounter as a parent. This is the situation we will use as an example to follow:

The school approaches you to discuss a particular issue they are facing with your child. It is a problem that needs to be addressed because it is disrupting the school's day-to-day routine. The school is very eager to discuss this problem with you.

At first glance, this seems like a pretty straightforward issue and you might already have a plan of action in mind for meeting with the school. This is where I will throw you for a loop.

What happens if the problem they are experiencing with your child at school does not happen at home? Is it still a problem? Is it your problem to deal with?

Once a "problem" has been identified, it is imperative to determine WHY it is a problem and WHO it is a problem for. Before I can elaborate on the why, I must clearly define WHAT a problem is.

How to define a problem

The most important thing to remember in this chapter is that a problem only arises when someone refuses to accept a situation or a change.

That is the only way a problem can exist. As long as everyone accepts a situation and is willing to work with it, there is no problem. There is only a problem once someone refuses to accept the situation.

With that being said, what may be a problem to you may not be a problem to someone else. A problem is only born once someone makes it a problem. That is a concept that is not easy to accept and to coexist with.

In the example we are using for this chapter, who is the person who is refusing to accept the situation or the change that needs to be made? What caused the behaviour in the first place and what changes are being made to make sure the behaviour does not happen again?

Before schools request a meeting with the parents to discuss the situation, attempts would have been made in class to remedy the situation. Where does the problem originate from? Is the child not taking well to the new plan? Is the teacher consistently following through with the plan? Is the school providing the necessary support the teacher needs?

Clearly, at this point, we can determine this is not the parents' problem. They are only being called in for support. This real issue to be addressed at this meeting now is to determine the source of the problem, in the most objective way possible. The parent should not feel blamed for this issue.

Why is it a problem?

When it comes to helping a child, once a "problem" has been identified, everyone involved must take the time to find out why it is a problem. Taking the situation given above, when the parents and the school meet to discuss the situation, this is the conversation that needs to happen:

- Why is that a problem for the child?

- Why is it a problem for the parents?

- Why is it a problem for the teacher?

- Why is it a problem for the school?

Before you can determine the why, you must first confirm that it is indeed a problem. Is it actually a problem for your child? Is it actually a problem for you, the parent? Is it actually a problem for the school?

As mentioned earlier, this process must be done in the most objective way possible. Often, this kind of situation will turn into a "finger-pointing" game between the adults, resulting in a poorly drawn up solution that does not take the child's needs into consideration.

This is where school trauma is the most damaging: when the adults get too caught up in their pride and ego to take accountability for their role in the child's behavioural outbursts, leading the child to believe that they are a very bad person.

Setting the intention for problem solving

When confirming the meeting with the school, make it clear that you wish to go over everyone's view on the problem, including your child's. This will lead the conversation in the direction it needs to go, moving away from the finger-pointing scenario that has no place in a child's support system.

Once everyone involved in the problem has identified how the "problem" affects them individually in their perspective realities, then you can move on to identify the true problem.

Starting off with an easier situation

Before we get into the complexity of the problem solving process of dealing with your child's poor behaviour at school, I am going to walk you through an easier issue you will encounter as a parent. The only reason why I identify this situation as "easy" is because it only involves you and your child as opposed to an entire educational team.

Let me put you in a situation where your child's room is constantly messy.

In this situation, we do not need to elaborate on why this is a problem. It just is! The when and where this is a problem has already been established so we can move on to the trickier parts.

We now move on to "who has the problem"?

Is this a problem for your child? Your first response may be to answer "yes" since it is your child who is not keeping their room clean. This is the trap we fall into as adults. Clearly, this is not a problem for your child since he or she is not bothered by the messy environment.

You however are about to lose your mind! We can confidently say that you have a problem with your child's messy room. The question now is: how are you going to address the issue without making it your child's problem?

Let's start off with why this is your problem. You want your child to understand the importance of keeping a clean environment but they just don't get it. Relating this to how we have seen the previous generations handle this situation, our initial thought would be to yell at our child and maybe even give them a consequence, or some type of punishment for having a messy room.

How effective is that approach? How well did it work on you? If it was the best way to handle this situation, why are children still keeping messy rooms? Shouldn't that be resolved by now?

Yelling, embarrassing, and berating your child will not resolve the issue simply because they do not understand your problem with it. They only understand that you are making it their problem.

This is the effective way to address the issue with your child:

You must first let your child know why their messy room is creating a problem for you and then ask them how they could help to resolve the issue. The process would look a little like this:

"You leaving a messy room makes me anxious and angry (or any other emotion you might feel), and it makes me feel disrespected. I know this is not your intention when you leave your room messy. Can you help me find a solution that will help us both?"

You can also add why it is important to keep a clean space but refrain from making it a lecture. They will not listen to you.

Although some of you may cringe at this approach, it has been proven effective. If the parent jumps right into the conversation by accusing and insulting the child of being ungrateful, the child will quickly shut off and claim that this situation is not his or her problem. And they are not wrong.

Getting your child involved in the solution also teaches them important life skills.

In finding the solution in this situation, ask yourself:

- Is the room set up to help my child keep it clean? Do we need to look at alternative storage solutions?

- Does my child understand what a clean room should look like? Did you ever show your child how to keep the room clean? What product to use? How to put the clothes away? What to use to dust and clean?

- Is it too overwhelming for your child? Start by breaking everything down into smaller tasks. Instead of saying "Clean your room," try saying, "Can you please pick up the clothes off the floor tonight?" Then move on to another task the following day, and so on.

- Not forgetting that our children do not listen to us (they imitate us), start looking at how clean the entirety of the house is. How tidy are the other rooms? What about the closet and other storage areas? How clean is the garage, the attic, the kitchen, the bathroom?

These are just some examples to get the ball rolling for you. You will know how to work it out accordingly with your child.

With these points cleared up, you are now able to work out a plan for your child to clean the mess, accept the fact that they may need your assistance in some areas, and then make a plan for how to maintain the room once the initial clean up is made.

Keeping this scenario in mind, let us go back to the initial issue with your child's behaviour at school.

When and where is it a problem?

Going back to the initial example for this chapter, let us say that the school claims your child disrupts the class continuously. It can easily be determined that this is a problem for the teacher. I would push this even further and ask, is it a problem for the class or just the teacher?

But can we be certain that your child actually disrupts the entire class? Or is your child simply disrupting the teacher who, in turn, focuses on it being a problem for the class?

This can open up quite a debate. A teacher who is tired and stressed out on a particular day will react to your child's disruptive behaviour quickly and demand an immediate course of action. But was the teacher in a position to have a good look at what caused the disruptive behaviour? Did the teacher check to see why your child was acting up? What was happening in the classroom that made your child uncomfortable to the point of displaying disruptive behaviours? Why did it become a problem?

Please note that I am in no way insinuating that the teacher is manipulating the situation. The reality is teachers are burned out, stressed, and overwhelmed. Any negative behaviours will eventually get to them.

In the situation we are following in this chapter, the school would back up the teacher and claim that the behaviour is a problem for the school because it is a problem for the teacher. But is it really disrupting the entire school? Unless your child displays the same disruptive behaviour outside of the classroom, the school cannot claim that it is a problem for the entire school.

You, as the parent, may not see it as a problem at all because, from your perspective, the behaviour would not happen if the child's needs were properly met in class. When and where is it an actual problem? We need to find the answer to that in the most objective way possible in order to be able to identify the true problem and therefore find the most effective solution.

In this particular example, the identified problem is that your child is disruptive in class. In order to find the right solution to this problem, it has to be the same problem for everyone involved.

In this case, the teacher's problem is that your child is bothering him or her in class. The school's problem is that the teacher is bothered. Your problem is that your child's needs are not being met in class.

Going through the process of identifying what the problem represents to everyone involved in this particular case has now broadened the root cause of the problem.

It is no longer the simple problem of your children disrupting the school. If this point is not addressed right away, everyone is looking for a solution that does not include everyone's reality of the problem. Everyone involved is now faced with a situation that has three different problems for three different points of view. And everyone is still missing something here.

Let me ask you the question again because this is the question everyone in this meeting will have to keep asking until a solution is found: What is the actual problem you are trying to solve?

Who has the problem?

Were your child's needs taken into consideration when the disruptive behaviour was displayed? Is your child included in the definition of the problem? So far, the example given here only touches on the adults' interpretation of the problem. So far, the problem stems from the adults, not the child. So why is the child labeled as the problem?

Once you have identified the adults' problem, you also need to look at the child's side of the "problem." When we are the ones facing the problem, we instinctively look for an outside source as the cause of that problem. We most likely are not ready to accept that we may be the only one with the problem.

This means that we are the ones who are not willing to accept the situation. Going with what the cause of a problem is, as stated above, we now become the one responsible for making this a problem. That is a hard pill to swallow.

Sorting it all out

So is your child the problem in this case? Was your child's behaviour really disruptive in class or was the teacher in a more irritable mood that day? If the behaviour was truly disruptive, what caused it? Could the disruptive behaviour have been provoked by something or someone in class? Was the disruptive behaviour a result of expectations not being made clear before an activity in class?

I am not suggesting that you completely disregard your child's behaviour here. There is something to be done to make sure your child understands that they are displaying unacceptable behaviours. What I am getting at is: did anyone look into what created the behaviour?

This is a good example of the unconventional approaches I have when it comes to finding a solution to behavioural issues. At first, people are not entirely comfortable with this approach because it forces them to look at the role they played in a child's behaviour.

I get the same reaction when dealing with conflicts between children. When the children I work with see me heading their way, they know what question I will be asking: "What did you do to get us here?"

The children know I am not accusing them of causing the problem. They know that I am simply holding them accountable for their part in it.

I have seen too many children get unjustly blamed, bullied, and shamed for behaviours that were provoked by the adults or other children. I have adapted my approach so that the children know I am standing up for them when it is necessary.

Do not get me wrong, if the root cause of the problem really is the child, then I will take that on and start working at how we can correct the behaviour.

So WHAT is the actual problem? Who is the player who is not willing to accept the situation or the change it requires?

WHY is it a problem? Why is this person not willing to accept the situation? It is with the answers you will get from these questions that you will find the right solution to the problem.

With this, you will have addressed the issue of whether or not everyone is working on solving the same problem. If it is determined that the problem really belongs to the teacher, then it is important to find the best ways to support the teacher to solve this additional source of stress.

How do you now put it all together?

Including your child in the solution

Getting your child's side of the story is important but that is not the only way to include them in the process.

As mentioned in the easier scenario of the messy room, your child will not necessarily understand what the big deal is. From their perspective, they usually feel a sense of injustice.

By mentioning to your child that his or her behaviour has a negative impact on the people around them and showing them that the adults are looking for their input on a possible solution, the lines of communication and cooperation are now open.

In this example, asking the child how they could change their behaviour to make it easier in class will open up the conversation. We need to consider the age and the maturity level of the child in this process. If the child is too young, the best approach is to draw up a plan to help the teacher, that the parent is comfortable with, and then explain to the child what the expectations are. This plan should also include step-by-step measures to help the child change the behaviour.

Identifying what everyone's role and responsibility is in the solution is also important. In this example, the parents can help with positive reinforcement that will encourage the child to maintain their good behaviours. The principal can review the plan with the teacher regularly to see if any additional support is needed and to make sure that the teacher is consistent with the steps of the plan.

To recap, here are some components to take into consideration when following this process:

- What is the problem (who is not accepting a situation)?

- Why is it a problem? What is the root cause of the problem?

- Is the problem really related to the child?

- When and where does this problem present itself?

- How does the problem present itself for everyone involved?

- Is it a problem for everyone involved?

- Is everyone working on a solution for the same problem?

- Is the child included in the solution?

- What is everyone's role in working on the solution?

No matter what the issue is, this process will solve it. You simply have to add the necessary factors at play and make the necessary adjustments for the situation you are dealing with.

It is important to note here that emotions cloud our interpretation of a problem. When emotions are running high and everyone involved has turned to the blame game, someone must recognize that this is only hurting the child. Adult problems should never be made a child's problem.

"We worry about what a child will become tomorrow, yet we forget that he is someone today."

- Stacia Tauscher

CHAPTER 8:
GETTING CLEAR
ON THE END RESULT

Another factor that is important to determine after identifying the real problem is: what everyone is looking to get out of the solution?

What do we all need in the end?

_____

When you start the process, it will become evident that there are only five things people seek. When those needs are not met, a problem arises. These needs are pretty much the same for everyone:

- The need to be heard

- The need to be seen

- The need appreciated

- The need to be recognized

- The need to be respected

Some may have other words to describe these needs but you will find that, most of the time, these other words are synonyms of the ones listed above.

In the world of children, negative behaviours arise when these needs are not met. If children do not feel heard or seen, they do not feel safe in their environment and therefore will act accordingly.

That is when adults are quick to label the child as problematic, but in this case, the adults are the problem. The adults are failing to provide a safe environment for the child to feel heard, seen, appreciated, loved, respected, and recognized as an individual.

> *When you welcome a child into your classroom or into your home, how are you showing up?*
> *How are you making him or her feel safe?*

The fascinating thing here is that the same needs are required by adults. We all feel the pressure to be the perfect parent, the perfect teacher, the perfect student, and the perfect child. We are all faced with the pressures of fulfilling the ideals that are expected of us.

We can agree that these ideals are not realistic. If a child is acting up in a classroom, the teacher will react according to the notion that if a colleague or a parent walks by at that particular moment, he or she will be judged as a teacher who does not have control of their classroom.

The same goes for parents. Have you ever been to the store where a child has a complete meltdown? If you are a parent, your reaction will be either that you are thankful it is not your child or that this particular parent is a bad parent. If you are not a parent, you will most likely believe that the parent does not have control of their child and are raising them badly. Parents are aware of this and react to the child's behaviour with the thought that they need to redeem themselves as parents.

With this reaction, the parent forgets that their child is communicating a need that is not being met. Every behaviour in a child is a form of communication. The negative behaviours, such as meltdowns, are a cry for help for something they cannot explain verbally.

Adults will have elaborate conversations about how children are manipulative or spoiled. No matter the situation, the child is only expressing that a need is not being met. The adult is then projecting what they do not wish to accept (the problem) onto the child rather than taking a moment to find the source of the problem.

I can tell you that, in such a situation, the child is not the problem. In the majority of the cases, it is the adult's problem that is creating a problem for the child.

Even with a child who is known to have behavioural issues, the meltdowns or negative behaviours are triggered by the adult. We cannot forget that. The child is not the problem. It is the adult's negative reaction to the behaviour that will teach the child the art of manipulation.

Once we approach a situation with the knowledge that the problem will not be interpreted the same for the people involved and that, in the end, we all want the same result, it takes no time at all to realize that we are all working for the same goal.

We need to work together to make it work. This is what has been lost over time, the "citizens" of the Village working together, not against each other.

The teacher complaining about a disruptive student is expressing that he or she is not being heard, seen, appreciated, respected, and recognized for the work they do. The parent, the school and the child are feeling the same in their own way. So why are they working against each other? Who is right and who is wrong?

Once we identify the real issue, find a solution that solves the problem for everyone involved, and understand that we all want the same end result, then the solution becomes crystal clear. No matter what the situation or the problem is.

The end goal will always need to be related to the well-being of the child... ALWAYS. If the solution is not showing improvements, it is because it was created to satisfy the adult's needs, not the child's. Once the end goal is to satisfy the child's need, the solution works every time.

By involving the child in the process, we are teaching them how to solve their own problems when they are on their own. This is a very important life skill that we need to pass on to our children.

Where the work begins...

This is a shorter chapter but just as important as all the others. When faced with a situation in which you believe that you will be judged for your child's behaviours, take a moment to assess the situation before reacting by going over the following points.

- What is my child trying to tell me?

- What need is not being met? (Are they tired, are they hungry, are they overstimulated, did you ignore the non-verbal cues that your child communicated to you, etc.)?

- How am I being triggered by this (were there days where this behaviour did not bother you in the past)?

- What could have been done to prevent this from happening?

- How can I model the desired behaviour to my child?

This is easier said than done as your parental triggers will be in full force in the heat of the moment. If you are not able to take a step back and react immediately, give yourself grace and go over the points once you have calmed down.

This is another muscle that needs to be worked: the detective work required to decipher your child's behaviours. Once you put this into practice, you will start to notice early on that you are able to detect those little, subtle, non-verbal cues your child sends out minutes or even hours before the behaviour manifests. You will be able to redirect or address the issue well before the problem arises.

I am not going to lie, this will make you feel like a Super Hero with incredible super powers! Embrace it!

"If we are to teach real peace in this world, and if we are to carry on a real war against war, we shall have to begin with the children."

- Mahatma Ghandi

CHAPTER 9:
THE NEXT CHAPTER

I am very much aware that the points I have addressed in this book may be difficult to digest at first. It took me a while and lots of practice to start feeling comfortable with the whole process. It is due to seeing the positive results over the years that I continue to introduce this concept to everyone I work and interact with.

For centuries, we have been conditioned to have our children conform to a specific system regardless of the negative outcomes.

The solution to our current issues with our youth cannot come from a place of resisting change.

We are still trying to create our future leaders by programming them as factory workers, forcing every individual to fit in the same box that is beneficial to this System.

We have reached a time, a shift from the old world to the new world, when we need to entertain different outlooks on how to move forward from here and make the positive changes needed for the new generations of world leaders.

The solution is not that difficult.

> *We need to stop expecting our children to conform to the system's needs. It is time for the system to conform to our children's needs.*

This will not result in chaos and it will not be the end of civilization as we know it. We are no longer raising factory workers who will be performing the same mindless task for the next 40 years. We are raising the next great leaders who will make positive changes to our world.

No matter where the child resides now, whether it is in an urban setting or in the middle of a mountain range, every child will now, at some point in his or her life, have to work with someone from a different country, with different traditions and different values.

We need to teach our children how to problem solve while respecting the needs of all other individuals. Remembering that we all want the same end result. We are all working for the same end goal... to end our time on this beautiful planet feeling accomplished and loved.

With my personal and professional experiences, it has become clear to me that this change does not require more work. The energy, time, and resources used to make the changes that will positively impact the future generations are the same that we are currently using now, trying to fight the changes that need to happen. Truthfully, it requires more work to keep fighting to fit our children in outdated boxes that no longer serve a purpose for the simple reason that we are uncomfortable with the change.

Moving forward, the relationship between a child and his or her Village needs to be one of partnership and mentorship. The parents need to create healthy partnerships with the members of the support system, the teachers need to create partnerships with the community to help each other, and most importantly, the child must be included in these partnerships.

In my 20+ years of working with children, I can honestly say that the children I worked with have taught me something every single day. They have so much to teach us, and we must allow them to be part of the solution.

We need to create an equilibrium between all the members of the community, all members of the Village, to uplift the child and give him or her an opportunity to bloom into the individual they are meant to be.

We can feel helpless when thinking about how we can make the world a better place for our children. Who are we to take on that challenge? Where do we even start?

The answer is a rather powerful one: you start with your own child.

It is not realistic to think that we can change the world all at once. It is however realistic to say that it can be done one child at a time.

This can be accomplished when every adult takes responsibility and accountability for their actions towards becoming great role models for all children.

The effect then grows exponentially as our children grow to be outstanding individuals, ready to take on the world with a much needed new approach.

This is how we get our children to surpass us in life.

CONCLUSION

The expression "it takes a Village" highlights that to truly support our children and create positive change, we must treat every child as we would our own. Instead of labeling children's behaviours as problematic, we should recognize that these behaviours mirror what they learn from us.

We must also stop judging parents based on their child's behaviour and acknowledge that without a strong support system—the Village—they are often just surviving. Similarly, we need to support educators who are doing their best with limited resources.

Psychology has shown that a child's social and emotional foundation is largely established within the first two years of life, meaning their future contribution to the world is shaped long before formal education begins.

By shifting our approach to parenting towards compassion, unconditional love, and inclusion, we can gradually make the world a better place, one child at a time.

ABOUT THE AUTHOR

Danielle C Baker, founder and CEO of Being Connected e-Learning Inc., is a passionate leader dedicated to empowering parents and educators. With over 20 years of experience, she is a Registered Early Childhood Educator, a TV talk show host, a podcast host, and an author.

Danielle also holds a B.Sc. in Physics from McGill University and has been teaching sciences to children for over 20 years. She specializes in creating programs for neurodiverse children and raising awareness to the specific needs of all individuals, ensuring that every child is given a fair chance to reach their full potential.

Through Being Connected, she offers workshops, courses, and resources designed to foster a nurturing and inclusive learning environment.

Outside of her professional life, Danielle enjoys connecting with nature and makes it her mission to bug her grown sons as often as she can!

She is committed to making the world a better place, one child at a time.

- Instagram: @danielleconnected

- TikTok: @danielleconnected

- Website: https://beingconnected.ca

- Email: danielle@beingconnected.ca

- More links: https://linkedtr.ee/danielleconnected

"A characteristic of the normal child is he doesn't act that way very often."

- **Author unknown**

"A person is a person, no matter how small."

- Dr. Seuss

thank you

Thank you for reading my book!

Dear Reader,

You made it to the end—thank you for walking this journey with me. I hope these pages offered you new insights, inspiration, and a deeper understanding of how we can work together to make this world a better place, one child at a time. Every connection we nurture, whether as parents, educators, or members of a community, brings us closer to creating a brighter future for the next generation.

If I could ask a small favor: if this book resonated with you, would you consider leaving a positive review on Amazon? Your thoughts could help others discover these ideas and join us in this mission of change and connection. Together, we can make a lasting impact.

Thank you for being a part of this dream. Your support means more than words can say.

Warmly,
Danielle

MY GIFT TO YOU

I am so glad you're here!

As my Gift to you, get FREE Access to the Audiobook of Bringing Up the World and other Free Book Bonuses by scanning the QR Code below or visiting https://beingconnected.ca/book

---

Made in the USA
Columbia, SC
19 February 2025

54120619R00096